PRAISE FOR SUCCESS WITHIN

"Knowing Lisa Wysocky as a publicist, a friend, and as a writer, I have seen her re-define herself reclaiming happiness and recapturing what could have easily been lost in the hustle-bustle of today's world. Using true life experiences, she has created a beautiful path to the success of spirit, and the infinite gift of fulfilling our heart's desires." **Devon O'Day, National Radio Host/SIRIUS and author of** *My Angels Wear Fur*

"Lisa Wysocky's *Success Within* is a roadmap for reinventing yourself, but it's also a step-by-step plan for molding a fine human being. It should be required reading for the human race." **Rick Lamb, syndicated radio host "The Horse Show" and author of** *The Revolution in Horsemanship* **and** *What It Means to Mankind and Horse Smarts* **for the Busy Rider**

"*Success Within* is loaded with unforgettable gems that are practical and vital. This refreshing book covers it all from thoughts, actions, and change, to giving, forgiving, and relaxing, to money, laughter, and much more. Success Within lights the way to ultimate success one week at a time. What a powerful concept!" **Carol Grace Anderson, M.A., author of** *Get Fired Up Without Burning Out*

"*Success Within* is a book straight from author Lisa Wysocky's heart. As I read it, it was almost as if she were beside me, gently urging me to incorporate her ideas to get those 'great moments' we all long for. In an often dark and negative world, *Success Within* shines through." **Danny Wright, "Danny Wright All Night," Jones Radio Networks**

D0910992

"We hosted a 'Wise Woman Retreat' in October 2004 and were fortunate to schedule Lisa Wysocky as a guest speaker. Her presentation, 'Success Within: How to Create the Greatest Moments of Your Life' touched on the value of setting goals, getting to know someone of a different generation or faith, volunteering, and more. Lisa captivated the entire room, moved many to tears, and earned a standing ovation. All are anxiously awaiting publication of this book." **Loudilla Johnson, co-president, The International Fan Club Organization**

"In *Success Within,* esteemed Nashville author and publicist Lisa Wysocky gives the reader a wonderfully powerful, user-friendly, 52-week road map to personal growth. Divided into four sections - `It's All In Your Mind,' `Treating Others Well,' 'Help Yourself,' and the concluding with `Bonus Round,' *Success Within* helps the reader experience `one year to a better, happier, more successful you.' Each of the easy-to-read 52 chapters (one per week), steps the reader through practical suggestions and advice based on the author's experiences or those of friends or colleagues. Wysocky's book is designed to be read one chapter a week, but she is such a gifted and fluid writer that many readers will devour it cover-to-cover the first weekend and then return to it weekly for the following 51 weeks." **Phil Sweetland, Country music and Radio contributor,** *The New York Times*

Success Within

Success Within

How to Create
the Greatest
Moments
of Your Life

LISA WYSOCKY

CHAMPION PRESS LTD.

BELGIUM, WISCONSIN

DEDICATION
★
To Colby—who graciously allowed
so much of his life to be discussed.
Thank you.

Other Books by Lisa Wysocky

The Power of Horses: True Stories from County Music Stars
Front of the Class (with Brad Cohen)

ACKNOWLEDGEMENTS

★

WORDS DO NOT express my deep appreciation to the following people: my agent, Sharlene Martin at Martin Literary Management; Brook Noel, Sara Pattow and the rest of the awesome crew at Champion Press; my son, Colby; and my mother, Pat.

Special thanks to Robert B. Parker who motivated me to write concisely. Thanks also to the many people who have inspired me, and to those who continue to, including: Carol Grace Anderson, Brad Cohen, Dale Franklin, Benita Hill, Loretta Johnson, Neville Johnson, Dhillon Khosla, Cindy Kubica, Kim McLean, Devon O'Day, Bill Royce, Preshias Tomes, Frosty Westering, John Wooden, and all the riders at Saddle Up! in Franklin, Tennessee.

TABLE OF CONTENTS

★

INTRODUCTION

✦

WOULDN'T IT BE great to live a tremendously successful life—a life that is immensely satisfying, and rich with rewards? Most people want that. Sounds good, doesn't it, to have everything you've always dreamed of? Well, you really can have it all. But first, you have to rid your mind of all your current ideas about success—the billions of dollars, the fancy cars, the mansions, the private island—and focus on true success, the success that is already within you. The end result will literally transform your life in more ways than you can possibly imagine.

We all need to be able to eat and pay our bills, so I am not discounting that money and the power that comes with it are a part of success. However, these attributes are a very small part of the success equation. *Merriam-Webster's Dictionary of English Usage* lists several definitions for success, one being "the satisfactory accomplishment of something attempted." "Something attempted" is some "thing" that you do. Any "thing." Going to the grocery store can be considered a successful "thing" that you did. But going to the grocery store usually does not create one of the greatest moments in your life. You have to learn how to turn that experience into a great moment.

Last year my friend Jennifer was very depressed following a nasty divorce. Her outlook on life changed from a sunny, positive view, to one of intense doom and gloom. I challenged her to say something nice to a stranger, to see if it made her feel any better. She said she couldn't possibly see how talking to a person she didn't know would lift her from the dark, miserable depths of her life, but she said she'd give it a try. A week went by and she had not made an attempt. Then another week passed. And another. Finally she said she'd talk to somebody just so I'd quit bugging her.

When Jennifer called me later that day, it was the first time I'd heard her happy in months. I'll let her tell the rest of the story.

I really didn't want to make the effort to say hi to a stranger. I mean, my husband had left me and my life was a mess. But then I thought, what the heck. I went to the store and tried making eye contact with several people, but I backed off after a few tries. For me, at this time in my life, this was harder than I thought it would be. But I had agreed to try, so I kept on. Three errands later at the post office, I found my stranger. She was a very elderly lady, shuffling along with a cane and dressed in a series of very worn and mismatched clothes. I stopped her by touching her arm and saying, "Excuse me." She looked up and just glared at me. I smiled and said, "I just wanted to tell you that your purple scarf looks beautiful on you." The old woman grasped my arm and began to cry. "Oh, I'm sorry, dear," she said through her tears. "You're so kind. I know I look a mess. My daughter died last week and I just can't seem to pull my life together. Everyone is treating me like I am a demented old hag. And I'm not, I am just very sad. You are the only person to say something nice to me in days. I will remember you kindly forever. Bless you."

Jennifer later said this was one of the greatest moments of her life. By reaching out, she made herself feel wonderful. Today Jennifer smiles and says hi to virtually everyone she passes. Just the simple act of passing along a smile has become very important to her. Additionally, her depression has lifted and she has been able to move on with her life.

It seems silly to think that a simple smile can change someone's world. But in the right circumstances, it can. A smile brings back to us a basic need—that of human kindness—and kindness has become very important to my friend Jennifer. What things are important to you? What do you value above all else?

In the last thirty years technology has totally rocked our world. Where every family used to have—or want—a bulky, expensive, dated encyclopedia, we now have up-to-date information regarding anything we can possibly think of free on the Internet. Where housewives used to spend hours planning, defrosting, and cooking a meal, anyone can now microwave food in thirty seconds or less. Technology has allowed us to replace our joints, do our banking—anytime--online, be able to talk to anyone—anywhere in the world—from our cars, and watch upwards of a hundred television channels, all at the same time.

Technology has provided us wonders beyond words, but it has also caused us to live in an immediate and superficial society. Our grandparents purchased quality furniture that would last their entire lives. Today we swap furniture as often as we do our cars. Today, what a person is wearing is often more important than who that person is. How much someone makes is more important than the integrity he or she displays while making it.

Our society as a whole has become so infatuated with money and material possessions that we have lost sight of those things that are really important—people. The events of 9/11 and the devastating tsunami in Southeast Asia brought home the realization that the only commodity that is really important in this world is the people who live in it. You. Me. Our sisters and brothers, parents and grandparents, friends and neighbors, and those whom we will never know. People.

Here's an example. If your home were burning, what would you save first? Tragedy has proven time and time again that the first thing you'd save are your loved ones inside. Your family. Then your pets, then your photographs. Your cell phone, your wallet, that new jacket you just bought, even your money—suddenly none of that is of any importance.

When push comes to shove, our priorities still do come into focus. What this shows is that although money is very nice, true success is really not about all the money you can make. It's about how you made that money. At the end of your life, if you had to choose, would you be more proud of closing that "big deal" or in raising a son who is productive in society? Would you get more enjoyment out of working overtime, again, or attending your granddaughter's ballet recital? Think about it. If you lived a life where you had to choose either/or, what would your choice be?

Let's face it. Not all of us are going to be millionaires. And those who have achieved that impressive milestone have no guarantee that all those zeros are going to bring them any amount of happiness, gratification, or peace. People are unfulfilled because they focus on the wrong areas. Success and happiness do not come from money, careers, big deals, and nice clothes. Success and happiness come from inside you, from what you do with your life and how you live it.

But how do you do that? How do you get out of the "keeping up with the Joneses" mentality and back to the important issues in life? How does one become happy and fulfilled while working fifty hours a week and raising a family—by yourself? How can you feel successful when helping an aging parent, battling chronic illness, or trudging week after week to yet another job interview? How can you feel good about stretching finances month after month to make ends meet, or any of the other issues we all have to deal with on a day-to-day basis?

As have many of you, I've lived all of that and more. I am not wealthy, but I am one of the richest people I know. Do I hope to have a bundle of material wealth someday? Of course, and there is nothing wrong with that. But I do not rely on money to dictate my success, or how I feel about myself.

Our true success is in how we treat others, and what we do with our lives. True success is determined by one thing and one thing alone: can you look in the mirror every night and know that you helped a fellow human being, made someone happy, and did the best you could with the set of circumstances you had to deal with that day? That's where you will find happiness and fulfillment and peace. Not in buying an expensive new car. Not in landing another sale. It is not external. It's inside. It's you.

And the best thing about being the best you that you can possibly be, is that good comes back to you. Great and unimaginable rewards come into your life—rewards you will remember forever as the greatest moments of your life.

Success Within is a fifty-two-week program broken into four different sections—It's All in Your Mind, Treating

Others Well, Help Yourself, and a Bonus Round—one year to a better, happier, more successful you. Each week features new elements for you to implement into your daily routine that will provide great moments in your life. Some of the weeks suggest short, quick exercises, other weeks contain exercises or tasks to be completed over time, but every one of them will change your life for the better.

You can begin *Success Within* anytime. Even today! But in this disposable society of ours, a year-long project may seem a bit intimidating. We are all conditioned to like and expect immediate results. That's okay. *Success Within* can help with that, too. If fifty-two weeks is a bit overwhelming, just pick one week, any week, and implement those specific elements. Implement all fifty-two weeks, and you will be amazed.

You can do *Success Within* by yourself, with a partner, with a group, or with your family—whatever works best for you. Sometimes you will finish the week's scheduled activities in a few days, other activities might stretch out over the course of several weeks, or even months. If you finish one week a little early, you can always go back and finish something left undone from a previous week.

I also suggest you keep a *Success Within* notebook or journal so you can easily refer to previous weeks' accomplishments. It can be a three-ring spiral notebook, a loose-leaf binder, a fancy scrapbook, or a series of pages you bind together yourself. The only important aspects are to have fun with it and make it yours. Feel free to be creative.

So, let us get to it. Let's go find your success. Let's go find the greatest moments of your life.

1

IT'S ALL IN YOUR MIND

Each of the thirteen weeks in this first section deal with your state of mind—you have to first believe you can do something before you can accomplish anything. Here you will learn to think positively, goal set, and appreciate what you have. Each week in Part 1—and in the other three parts as well—features a "success plan" that can be incorporated into your life that week. Part 1 sets the stage mentally and physically for all the memorable moments that will soon follow.

Week 1

IF YOU THINK YOU CAN, YOU WILL

*"Whether you think you can or you think you can't,
you're absolutely right."* —Henry Ford

The power of positive thinking has been documented time after time. Generally speaking, it's the belief that you can conquer the world, if only you believe that you can. It's the idea that if you believe in yourself, if you have determination, courage and competitive drive, you can accomplish just about anything. It's Peter Pan and Wendy, flying because they think they can. They believe.

Of course, people can't really fly, but we can all accomplish great things. In my younger days I was a horse trainer. My first year on the professional horse show circuit, I won a reserve world championship. I didn't play the political game. I didn't wine and dine judges or place expensive ads in the program books. I just worked very hard and did the very best that I could do. I did well because I believed I could. I had brought that horse to the peak of her training the day of the world championships and did well because no one ever told me that I couldn't. I later found that even though a lot of people were rooting for us as true underdogs, no one else believed we could win without a lot of dollars and political moves. Luckily, my mind never entertained the thought that I couldn't be in the top few placings and "it will never happen" changed to "the impossible just happened."

One thing that holds us back is the lack of belief in ourselves and in our goals. Like Peter Pan and Wendy, we have to believe. Positive thinking can be more difficult for some than for others. Many are conditioned from birth to believe that no good will ever come to them. But there are countless success stories out there of people who have come from nothing, only to become household names and role models to us all. The only way that can be achieved is if you believe in yourself. There are others who have endured horrendous physical and mental horrors, who have gone on to be an inspiration to millions of people.

Helen Keller is a prime example. Illness robbed her of her sight and hearing when she was a toddler, yet she went on to become a world-renowned author and teacher. Helen went to college, wrote nearly a dozen books, traveled all over the world, met twelve United States presidents, and lived to be eighty-seven. That took an incredible amount of guts and courage, especially as she lived during a time when those with disabilities were often put in institutions, and lived a very bleak existence. Helen Keller believed.

Another example is the legendary jockey Eddie Arcaro, who lost two hundred fifty races before he ever came across the finish line first. How many of us would have had the drive, determination and belief in ourselves to continue after such a long losing streak? But Eddie Arcaro so believed in himself, he not only convinced himself he was a great jockey, he convinced trainers and owners to let him ride their horses. I can only wonder, if I owned a racehorse, and a jockey who had lost over two hundred races—and never won a single race—asked to ride my horse, would I have let him? What would he have had to say or do to convince me that there was a chance he'd bring my horse home in the money?

Apparently Eddie Arcaro convinced a great many people, because he went on to win horse racing's prestigious Triple Crown—not once, but twice. Additionally, he won the Kentucky Derby five times, the Preakness and Belmont six times each, won a total of 4,779 races and over $30 million in purses. Upon his retirement, *Sports Illustrated* called him "the most famous man to ride a horse since Paul Revere." Eddie Arcaro believed.

Imagine the great moments that Helen Keller and Eddie Arcaro must have had during their lives. What adventures Helen must have had traveling around the world and meeting a dozen presidents! And how proud and happy Eddie must have felt when he won the Triple Crown for the first time—and the even greater thrill when he won it again!

Yes, money was a part of it. But when Helen Keller was in her eighties, do you think she was proud that a certain book she wrote brought her so many thousands of dollars, or would she think fondly of all the places she went, all the people she met, all the lives that book changed for the better? Do you think Eddie Arcaro was more excited about his 10 percent of the purse money, or the fact that he was the first man in the history of the world to win the Triple Crown—twice?

Before you begin creating some of the greatest moments of your life, you have to believe in yourself. You have to believe you can. As the old adage says, "You can't spell success without U." You have to believe.

We've all heard variations of the story of the young man and the calf. A young man goes out to the barn and lifts a newborn calf. The calf weighs less than a hundred pounds, so we know the young man is in good shape. However, many young men can lift that amount without too much trouble, so the feat is not all that spectacular. Well, every day for weeks and months the young man goes out and lifts the calf. And, as calves tend to do, every day the man went out to the barn, the calf had grown a little bigger. And as the months passed, the calf grew from less than a hundred pounds to well over three hundred pounds. Yet the young man still lifted that calf because he believed he could. No one had ever told him, "You can't lift that calf. That calf is too big." So the young man believed.

You then have to look at the other side of the story. How many three hundred pound calves are going to allow themselves to be lifted into the air? The calf allowed himself to be lifted every day because he, too, believed. The calf believed that the young man could lift him, as it had been done every day of the calf's life.

You are a unique individual. No one, not even if you are an identical twin, has your exact personality, features, thoughts, and life experiences. Everyone on this planet is special, and has special gifts. Maybe yours, like my friend Jennifer's, is sending a smile out to everyone she meets. Maybe yours is nurturing your kids, or making money to support your family, or championing the elderly, or teaching children how to read, or delivering the mail. The possibilities are as unique and different as we all are. Know that no matter who you are, you are different, you are special, and you are needed as an important member of our society. Those are all wonderful attributes.

How do you find such strong belief in yourself that you, too, believe that you can lift your own version of that three hundred pound calf—especially on days when life kicks you in the teeth? How do you find this self-confidence? It can be done in just a few easy steps every day.

Step 1: Find Time

We all are busy. Sometimes it seems as if our lives control us, rather than the other way around, but it is important to devote time every day to work on the steps I will outline. It doesn't have to be a large chunk of time. If quiet and privacy are an issue, take five minutes in the car after you've dropped the kids at school. Get up five minutes early. Spend an extra five minutes in the bathroom. Work faster and cut five minutes from your daily housecleaning. Even the busiest people can find five minutes *if they really want to.* You can do this. Be creative and you can make it work.

Step 2: If You Believe in Yourself, Your Body Will Show it

Whether in movies or in real life, we have all seen the visual image of the poor, downtrodden soul—shoulders drooping, head down, slow, shuffling walk. The world has beaten every bit of hope out of him. Then there is the person who has the world by the tail. You easily recognize her from her brisk pace, her shoulders thrown back, head held high. By adopting the most confident body posture possible, she is showing the world that she believes in herself. Those around her will begin to relate to her as a strong and confident person, and that in turn will bring even more confidence back to this young woman.

To develop a new posture, and a new attitude to show the world, you have to remember to stand tall and face the world like a winner. For anything to be effective, you have to be pro-active in implementing it. And with the different directions our lives pull us each day, it is easy to slip back into old habits. So write a note to yourself that says:

TODAY I WILL STAND TALL
AND FACE THE WORLD LIKE A WINNER

Write the note now, and put it in a place where you will see it often—on your computer monitor, your refrigerator, your phone receiver—any place where you will see that note often throughout each day from now on.

Step 3: Visualize Your Success
Choose a goal, any goal, then take a quiet moment alone and visualize yourself successfully completing the goal. This technique is often used in professional sports. The theory is if you visualize the successful attempt of an activity before actually doing it, you are more likely to succeed. For example: basketball players of all levels might shoot basketball free throws in two different ways. In the first, the free throws might be shot as one would normally on the basketball court. In the second, an athlete might close his eyes and visualize himself taking—and making—the shot.

Stan Kelher, a former men's basketball coach at C.W. Post University in New York is one of many who has successfully used visualization techniques for his teams. Some years ago, he wrote a book, *Basketball Cybermetrics*, which is about preparing mentally for all areas of the game, especially shooting. Coach Kelher was a visualization expert. His theory was simple. If players could visualize, for example, successful shooting, their overall skill in that area would be improved. Kelher would have his players do nightly free throws in the gym, but when the player went home, the last thing he'd do before closing his eyes was to visualize the free throw and see the ball going into the basket.

This visualization exercise can be done anywhere—in an airplane, while taking a walk, during a quiet break at the office. And you don't have to be a basketball player for it to work. The goal visualized can be anything from sailing through a job interview, to successfully negotiating household chores with your teenager, to losing twenty or thirty or more than a hundred pounds.

Let's say your goal is to exercise more. You hate exercising, but know for health reasons that it needs to be a regular part of your day. Take five and sit somewhere quietly. Now close your eyes, and visualize yourself exercising. As an example, let's say you are taking a walk around your neighborhood. Look at the clothes you are wearing and how great they look on you. Hear the sounds around you. Realize how nice it is to be outside, and away from the phone for a few minutes. Feel your blood pumping and the cholesterol in your veins disappearing. Be amazed at how wonderful your body is feeling. Experience in your mind the rhythm of the walk. You are walking faster and faster and faster and you feel great!

So choose a goal for yourself—something that's been difficult for you to accomplish. Then every day, visualize the successful completion of your goal, while you take actual steps to complete it.

Week 1 Success Plan

* Whatever it is that you want to do, believe that you can
* Find five minutes every day
* Write the note, "TODAY I WILL STAND TALL AND FACE THE WORLD LIKE A WINNER" and place it where you will see it often
* Take time every day to visualize the success of your new goal
* Make an effort to reach the goal

ALLOW YOURSELF TO DREAM

"Hold fast to dreams for if dreams die, life is a broken winged bird that cannot fly."—Langston Hughes

Remember back in high school when you were going to change the world? You were going to find a cure for the common cold, be a rock star, or simply marry the man—or woman—of your dreams.

So . . . um . . . what happened?

We all have dreams, but unfortunately very few people ever take the time to make their dream a reality. Maybe your dream is to become a doctor. Maybe it is to sail around the world, or start a business, or become debt free. Or, your dream could be much simpler. Maybe your dream is to start a family, land the perfect job, finish school, or is as basic as re-organizing your spare closet.

When I was a child, I thought nothing could be cooler than to drive a big truck. It's a simple dream, but for a girl in the 1960s, it was a dream that was strongly discouraged— discouraged by everyone, that is, except my mother. She raised me to believe anything was possible.

As I got older, my dream of driving a truck faded. Now I wanted to train horses. There were many obstacles in my way, but I got through them one by one and eventually landed my dream job. As I traveled around the country showing horses, I had a lay-over one day at a stable close to my mother's Minnesota home. When my mother arrived in the midst of us unloading, she became very excited.

"You finally did it!" she cried.

"Did what, Mom?" I questioned, my eyes still on the unloading process.

"Your first dream," she said. "Remember you always wanted to drive a big truck? Well, just look at your rig. There is your dream. You did it!"

I pulled my eyes toward the huge truck and nine-horse trailer I was driving and realized she was right. I was driving a great big truck, and you know, it was every bit as much fun as I had always dreamt it would be. I had worked very hard to be a horse trainer and hauling horses in a big truck across the country was a necessary part of showing on a national level. I mentally gave myself a high–five as I went back to the horses, for after all, how many people actually get to realize their earliest ambition?

Some people have many dreams, while others have one primary dream. For whatever reason, most people never see their dreams come true. Worse yet, many people never even try to attain their dreams.

The reasons for not achieving—or trying—are many. Some people get a job, marry, and have children. Some become single parents, or are busy caring for relatives. Some who try are unfocused. They have a dream, but aren't quite sure how to get there. Others are easily discouraged, or lose their motivation.

I used to be one of those busy, easily distracted people. For many years I had wanted to write a book. I actually started a few times, but as a single parent who worked a full-time job, my time was limited. I was busy taking my son to after-school activities. I had to clean the house. The yard needed mowing. I had laundry to do. The dog had to go to the vet. My excuses were endless.

Then one summer day while driving my son to Boy Scout camp, I caught the tail end of a radio interview with popular suspense writer Mary Higgins Clark. She was talking fondly, not of the thrills of mega-authorship, or fame and fortune, but of the early days of her writing—of late nights and early mornings and juggling writing with her kids and all the housework. Her emotional voice shared how her family pulled together to help her find time to write, and she spoke proudly of the encouragement she received from her children.

Then Mary Higgins Clark changed my life. Mary mentioned that when she began writing, she was a working, widowed mother of five, and if she could find time to write, then anyone could find time to write. That statement hit me right where it hurt. The very next day, I began waking an hour earlier every day to write. It was slow going, but eight months later, I had a finished book. With the words of Mary Higgins Clark still fresh in my mind, I found an agent who found a publisher, and the book was published. Since then I have written several books, but none of them would have seen the light of day without Mary Higgins Clark to nudge me along. So Mary, wherever you are, thank you.

Whether or not your dream is to write a book, hopefully Mary's words will stay with you as you commit to making your dream a reality. Dreams are not like fairy tales. They don't magically come true without some effort on your part. But remember, where there is a will, there is a way. If a widowed, working mother of five can turn into a best-selling novelist, you too, can achieve your wildest dream.

Fred Smith, founder of the overnight delivery service

FedEx, used his vision of the overnight delivery idea as a model for a college term paper. His professor was skeptical that such a company could be profitable and gave the paper a "C." Fortunately, Fred Smith didn't think much of the assessment. He believed strongly in his dream, proceeded forward, and risked all he had. Fred was hours away from bankruptcy when his funding finally came through. The rest, as they say, is history.

Some dreams, like Fred Smith's, are of specific, big business ideas. Others are not as easily defined.

Noted political leader Martin Luther King just wanted people—all people—to be treated fairly. Dr. King was born in the 1920s in Georgia, the son of a minister and a schoolteacher. He had a dream of a colorless society—a society where a person's worth was based on performance, not the color of their skin. He knew that to achieve his dream he would have to take certain steps. He would have to get an education. He would have to find others with similar beliefs and dreams. He would have to learn to speak well in public to get his ideas across, to raise funds to help accomplish his goals, to learn about legal matters to help introduce and change laws. Dr. King did not live to see the realization of his dream, but think how much closer we are today than when he was a child.

Martin Luther King, Fred Smith, Mary Higgins Clark and countless others who have achieved their dreams are not much different than you are. Not much, but a little. These differences are small, but very, very important.

First difference: they tried. It's as simple as that. These people made a firm commitment to their dream and tried to the best of their ability to make it happen.

Second, and more importantly, each person was able to achieve because he or she knew how to break the dream into manageable parts. This is important. You will not realize your dreams and create great moments until you are able to divide your dream into workable parts.

Let's say you have a simple dream. Maybe you are one half of a young married couple with children and you'd like to go to college. It's a simple wish, wanting to get an education, but circumstances often turn simple things into the nearly impossible. Two obstacles might be time and money. How do you overcome these obstacles to achieve your dream? Begin by breaking the dream into manageable parts.

Here are a few steps you might take to make this dream a reality:

* Check local colleges to compare subject matter and costs. Community colleges or technical colleges might be a low-cost option.
* Find out what grants, loans or scholarships you might qualify for—you may be surprised at what is out there.
* Redo your household budget to see what you can afford. Most households can reduce costs, if needed.
* Check with parents or relatives to see if they can offer financial help.
* Look around the house to see what you can sell to pay for tuition. Have a yard sale, sell the extra television, or take gently worn clothing to a consignment shop.
* Can't afford an entire semester? Take one or two classes.
* Discuss childcare with your spouse, neighbors, friends and relatives. You will be encouraged at the number of

people who will jump in if they know they are helping with your education.

* Get a copy of the semester calendar.
* Choose a class.
* Think how proud you will be on your graduation day.
* Go for it!

Can you do all of this in one day? Of course not. But if you devote a few minutes a day to this effort, every day, you will see significant progress after just a few days.

Each dream is distinctive, simply for the fact that it is your dream. So let's take this concept one step further and develop a real plan, one that will help you achieve all you have ever dreamed.

Step 1: Develop a "Dreams" List

Get several letter-sized sheets of paper, and label one of the pages "Dreams." On this page, list all of the wildest ideas you have ever had. This is the page for the really big dreams, the ones you have always talked about, but knew deep down, you'd never accomplish. These are the goals that will take years to reach. Your list might include ideas such as: climbing Washington state's Mt. Rainier, hiking the Appalachian Trail, building your dream home from the ground up, or getting a doctorate in your favorite subject.

Go crazy with this list. Think of all the fun this world has to offer that you'd like to experience. Some people go all out and even cut pictures out of magazines to illustrate their dream, or decorate their list with yarn and glitter. Just make it yours. When you are done, put the list where you will see it often.

Step 2: Develop a "Desires" List

Now title the second sheet of paper "Desires." This list consists of items that are achievable within a year or two, if you work hard. Dreams on this list might be: learning to snowboard, becoming debt free, writing a book, taking a big vacation, organizing a family reunion, or taking your business to another level.

Again, give your mind free rein and have fun decorating the list. These lists will probably take several days or more to complete since you will likely think of additional dreams and desires. Hang it next to the "Dreams" list when you are done.

Step 3: Develop a "Goals" List

Finally, you are to the "Goals" list. This is the list of all the little things you can get done in the next few months. Cleaning closets, landscaping your yard, starting piano lessons, taking the family to the zoo, exploring a nearby town, having a family movie night at home, organizing a pajama party, learning to roller blade, or taking a computer class are goals that might be on this list. This is the last list you will decorate, so go all out. Be sure to hang it with the other two lists.

Step 4: Take Action

Now you are ready to begin. Choose something from your "Goals" list, and in your *Success Within* notebook itemize all the steps you need to take to make that specific goal happen. For example, if one of your goals is to take a train trip, you'd need to check train schedules and costs, figure out how to pay for the trip (maybe your savings, or getting a second job, or selling an unneeded piece of furniture), decide where you'd like to go, choose the day(s) for the trip, have some idea of what you'd like to do when you reach your destination, and find a place to stay if you are taking an overnight trip. Remember to bring your camera!

As you accomplish each item on the list, cross it out or, if you like, put a little gold star by it. When you finally take your trip, add a big star next to where the trip is listed on your "Goals" list. Before too long, your "Goals" sheet will be full of stars, and your life will be full of great moments.

You'll find that as you move through your goals, you'll begin working on specific steps to make your desires happen. Remember to visualize your goals every day. Then, as your desires become realities, you'll begin achieving some of your dreams. Before too long, you'll be making new lists, because your original lists are full of gold stars, and you'll have a whole new set of ideas to explore, and experiences to remember.

Week 2 Success Plan

* Make a list of your wildest dreams
* Make a list of objects and achievements that you desire
* Make a list of your immediate goals
* Place the lists where you will see them often
* Visualize your success
* Take regular and specific steps to accomplish the goals

Week 3

TOTAL RECALL

"[Memory is] a man's real possession . . . In nothing else is he rich, in nothing else is he poor." —Alexander Smith

One of my favorite memories from childhood is of my mother, grandmother, and me listening to Minnesota Twins baseball on the radio. I can see the sunlight shining in through the partially closed drapes, and the dust mites swirling in the light. I am maybe five or six, and I am sitting on the floor, on a rough, dark blue carpet playing with my model horse collection. For some reason I know that it is a Sunday afternoon, late spring or early fall, but the windows are closed so it's not during the heat of the summer. My mother is on the couch to my right, embroidering something, and my grandmother is sitting to my left in a chair by the big picture window smoking a cigarette and drinking a glass of beer.

It's not a very dramatic memory, but I get a very warm, safe, and loved feeling whenever I recall that particular moment. It's a moment that I doubt was memorable for my mother or grandmother, but for me it was special. And that's what this week is all about, remembering those special moments that are meaningful, if only to you.

Memories are a huge part of our lives. In many ways, experiences—which become memories—shape who and what we are. If you are to create great moments in the future, you have to remember great moments of the past. For some, this is harder to do than for others. Many people have a hard time remembering. Others have unfortunate experiences in their past that they'd just as soon forget. What is needed this week are the activities or moments in your past that made you feel safe and warm and loved. Think back. What made you happy? What made you jump up and down with excitement? What moments were so special they brought tears to your eyes?

In the course of my career as an entertainment publicist, I have had the opportunity to write hundreds of bios for entertainers of all genres. One of my public relations clients was the legendary country music star Johnny PayCheck. John was best known for his 1978 hit, "Take This Job and Shove It," which happened to be written by another former client of mine, David Allan Coe. I did John's public relations in the early 1990s, and back then John loved a good meal. If I wanted a long career discussion with John, I found he was most forthcoming across the dinner table.

I remember asking John about his earliest memory. We were at one of his favorite restaurants, the Country Buffet in Goodlettsville, Tennessee, just north of Nashville. I was gathering information for his "fact sheet" (a promotional piece of quick bits of trivia information that often accompanies a bio). He started with a memory at school when he was about ten, then moved to a scene at a country store when he was seven or eight, and finally recalled playing with a dog when he was maybe four or five. What I remember most about John telling me the dog story was the look of pure happiness on his face. As he remembered, it was as if he was transporting himself back to a time when life was simple. It was a time when the act of throwing a stick for a dog brought pure joy, and just recalling the memory brought those joyous feelings back to him. He smiled through the rest of the meal, remembering that dog and the fun they'd had.

This week's success plan is to recall those great moments of your past. Then you'll explore those moments as much as possible with the people or places that were a part of it.

Step 1: Remember

To begin remembering, you might try to recall your first memory and take your life year by year from that point. Or you might find memories from a central theme in your life, say football, or girl scouts, or family vacations; or you could find memories from certain places you lived, or schools you went to, or people you knew. There are many ways to trigger memories. Looking through a photo album might trigger memories, or holding an object that was important in your past. Just find your personal trigger to start the flow of memories. Remember to "ink what you think"—to write the memories down so you remember them!

When thinking about these memories, try to bring back all the details that you can. What time of year was it? Was it hot or cold? Was it sunny or rainy? What were you wearing? What colors are in the memory? What smells or sounds or tastes? Who, if anyone, was there with you? Were you happy or sad? Be sure to record all of these details in your *Success Within* notebook.

As you go through this process, some memories are going to be more vivid than others. Some will be vague impressions, while others will be very clear in your mind. Some memories you will recall with delight, while others might be of sadder times. Whatever the memories, there will be a few that will become your favorites. These memories are the ones you will focus on next.

Step 2: Revisit

By now you should have recalled a dozen or more great moments. Choose one or two that are special to you, then make plans to revisit the moment more completely. For example, if you remember going shopping for school clothes with your mother, ask her about that time. What was going on in her mind at that point in her life? Was she worried about not having enough money for the clothes? Or was she pressed for time, or using the day to talk to you about other things? View the memory from her side.

Maybe you once made the winning shot in a basketball game—in overtime. Look up your old teammates and relive that day. Or make plans to visit your old high school and walk down memory lane. If that's not possible, how long has it been since you visited a basketball court? Go shoot some hoops, or teach someone else how.

Understand that it is very possible that other people involved in your memory won't remember the event at all. And that's okay. But be sure to share what you remember and why the memory, and your friend's part in it, mean a great deal to you. Even if he doesn't remember, you will make him feel very good by knowing he contributed in some small way to a great moment in your life.

The other possibility is that he will have a completely different memory of the event. Talking with other people about your recollection is a wonderful way to get to know another side of someone, and hear how the event was important in their life. The other person may also be able to add new information to the memory, enriching it even further.

If you don't have anyone from those special times in your life to reminisce with, find a memory partner. Choose one day each week or month to share memories with each other. This person could be a spouse, a child, a neighbor or co-worker. It could be a man you ride the bus with to work, or a woman from your church. The only requirement is that he or she has the desire to listen and share his or her own memories.

Step 3: Find a Daily Memory Moment

In addition to recalling and exploring great memories from your past, take time every day this week to create a daily memory moment. If you see a rainbow, stop and appreciate its beauty. Take a moment to enjoy watching the mime on the street, to smile at kids playing tag, or simply enjoy the graceful lines of a building.

I once dated a man whose greatest memory of our relationship is most likely a walk in the park on a snowy day. We briefly spotted the scarlet brilliance of a cardinal against the snowy backdrop. It was a breathtaking moment and it struck something deep within him. Regardless of his feelings about me, I am sure he will remember that moment fondly and forever.

Another client of mine lost his wife in a tragic suicide. In the weeks and months that followed he mentioned to me several times that the only thing that got him through were the special moments that each day brings: the beauty of a tree, the song of a bird, the lazy movement of clouds in the sky, a smile on someone's face.

So each evening this week, take a moment and jot down your greatest special memory of the day.

Week 3 Success Plan

* ★ Recall some of the great moments of your past
* ★ Revisit those moments with the people or places important to that moment
* ★ Find a special moment every day to cherish

WEEDING "STUFF" FROM YOUR LIFE

"You can never get enough of what you don't need to make you happy." —Eric Hoffer

I once knew a guy who had close to three hundred T-shirts. Now these weren't collector shirts with fancy logos or pictures of places he had visited. These were your standard black, white, green, navy or gray 100 percent cotton T-shirt. Most of the shirts he had never worn, and never would. This same guy also had six large boxes of band-aids in his bathroom cabinet, and bought toothpicks in bulk. I mentioned that maybe it would be a good idea to donate some of the T-shirts to the Goodwill, or a homeless shelter where someone who really needed them could use them, but he couldn't bear to part with a single one. Dave Ramsey, syndicated radio host and author of *Financial Peace*, has a term for this kind of behavior. It's called "stuffitis."

We live in a consumer driven society. Every hour of every day we are convinced by very savvy marketers that we need a bigger sofa, more long-distance minutes, improved gutters on the house, a new car, and yes, a super-sized fast food meal. We are bombarded day after day, hour after hour, minute after minute. It's no wonder we buy "stuff" we do not really need.

Not everyone is afflicted with "stuffitis" as badly as my friend, but everyone has possessions they no longer—or never—use. In addition to giving unused or unwanted items to those who desperately need them, there is a philosophy that states that clearing clutter from your surroundings clears your mind.

No one knows that better than Judy Hope, a Nashville-based graphic designer. Years ago, just a few days before Christmas, her house burned to the ground. Except for her car and her purse, she lost every material possession she had in the world. She was understandably traumatized and months later would look for a particular item of clothing in her closet, or a pan from her cupboard, only to realize it had burned in the fire. But Judy once told me that as traumatic as losing everything was, it was also a very freeing experience. She chose to use the tragedy as an experience in growth, reasoning that she had been given a rare opportunity to rebuild her life from the ground up. She now is happier and more fulfilled than ever before.

Judy realized that happiness is not found in material possessions. When push comes to shove there are very few material goods that are important in life. "Stuff" is nice to have, but having stuff does not make a person happy. Some stuff can make people's lives more comfortable. But stuff is not necessary for happiness or fulfillment.

The movie *Cast Away*, starring Tom Hanks, is another example. In the movie, Hanks' character is stranded on a deserted island for several years. His one sole possession is a soccer ball he names Wilson. Throughout the movie, Hanks' character grows and matures—all without the benefit of TiVo, palm pilots . . . and one too many T-shirts.

I'm not saying that you should get rid of things by burning down your house or isolating yourself on a desert island! Nor should you toss your son's third grade artwork, or mementos that have meaning for you. But this week focuses on cleaning out closets, basements, garages, cabinets, drawers and every other place that is host to items you do not use or need. You will also learn to resist the subtle and not so subtle pitches that encourage you and your money to part ways.

Step 1: Make it Fun!
For some, going through piles of "stuff" can be a daunting task, so it is important to make it fun. Invite some friends over to help and make a party out of it. (Be sure to return the favor some day and help them, too.) Or turn on some music and dance your way through the project. Go wild! Do you really need the velvet Elvis painting in the basement, or the beanbag chair with the rips in it? Get rid of them.

When you are finished, you will have an impressive pile of possessions that you really don't need, and you will have had a great time.

Step 2: Get Rid of it
It is then your choice to 1) hold a yard sale and convert some of the unwanted items to cash, 2) donate the pile to a worthy charity, or 3) sell high-dollar items at a deep discount.

Yard sales, by the way, are great fun and you meet a lot of very interesting people. It is a wonderful feeling to watch potential customers smile as they find something they need in your pile of outcasts. Whoever would think that you could have one of the greatest moments of your life at a yard sale? But it could happen! There are people out there who really do need what you don't.

You could make the sale a bigger event by asking neighbors to join in, or by putting an ad in your local newspaper. If you're not that organized you can just throw stuff out on the front lawn. I guarantee people will find you! People who buy regularly at yard sales have a sixth sense of where the sales are. If you are an apartment dweller and don't have a yard, ask a friend with a house to do a joint sale, or maybe your church, company, or school group would want to do a group sale on their grounds. Where there is a will, there is a way.

If you're not up for a yard sale, know that some charities pick up donated items, and most will give you a receipt so you can deduct the value of the donation from your taxes. You might also try a combination of the two by donating the remains from the yard sale.

If you have high-ticket items, you can sell them through a newspaper ad or to a pawn shop. Selling higher ticket items over the Internet is also an option. Amazon.com, and eBay are just two of the many online sites that offer possibilities for turning unwanted objects into cash.

Step 3: Resist Temptation

Remember that savvy marketers bombard you every hour of every day. Marketers don't really want you to buy their product. They just want your money. These salespeople are trained—and very well, I might add—to come between you and your hard-earned cash.

But you can foil their efforts by buying only what you absolutely need. In fact, in order to avoid replacing all the "stuff" you just spent a few days getting rid of, I challenge you to see exactly how much you can live without. Every day this week when you are making a purchase, ask yourself if you really need the extra-large double-vanilla cinnamon latte. Does your eight-year-old son really need (another) action figure? Are you buying that cute sweater set as a gift for your sister, or is it really for yourself? At the end of the week, make a list of all the items you didn't buy and add up the dollar amount you saved. Chances are, you'll be very surprised.

Now comes the fun part, take the amount you saved and put it to good use. You could pay some bills, donate it to your favorite charity, take an old friend to lunch, or begin saving for a family vacation. Your choices are endless and far more meaningful than purchasing another item you really didn't need.

Step 4: Your Daily Pick

Lastly, at the end of each day, choose one item that helped you get through the day. What one thing was it that you absolutely, positively could not have done without? Maybe it was the car that helped get you to work; maybe it was the alarm clock that woke you up on time, or the computer that gave you your daily assignments via email. Maybe it was a mail carrier who brought a check that paid your rent, or it could simply be a kiss from your wife that saved an otherwise unsalvageable day.

In your *Success Within* notebook, create a "Daily Pick" list. Every day add one item that helped you through your day. Just one. Every day. After a week—or a month—the list will weed out the "stuff" in your life from the necessities that are truly important to you.

Week 4 Success Plan

* Sort through those things that you have no use for and get rid of them
* Avoid buying new "stuff"
* Pick one item every day that was essential in getting you through your day

Week 5

CHOOSE HAPPINESS

"Happiness is not in the mere possession of money; it lies in the joy of achievement, in the thrill of creative effort."
—Franklin D. Roosevelt

Have you seen the picture of the elderly lady wearing a purple hat and flying a kite? I can't wait to be her. She obviously is having the time of her life and has enough self-confidence to do what makes her happy—no matter what others think. She's definitely a lady who thinks her cup is half-full, versus being half-empty.

Is your cup half-empty or it is half-full? I recently wrote a book with a man named Brad Cohen, who a few years ago was Georgia's First Year Teacher of the Year. That is quite an accomplishment on it's own, but if you add in the fact that Brad has Tourette Syndrome, a disabling condition that causes uncontrollable facial spasms and vocal outbursts—such as "Woop, woop" and "Jah . . . jah . . . JAH"—every few seconds, Brad's accomplishment becomes truly astounding.

How must it be for Brad, to go through life with his face constantly contorting into strange grimaces, his neck jerking back and forth, and strange sounds popping out of his mouth? Brad will tell you his life is wonderful.

But how can that be? It is difficult, if not impossible for Brad to do the countless daily activities many of us take for granted—such as going to a movie, or the library, or a concert. Brad has been beaten by strangers, and thrown out of restaurants for a neurological disorder that he can't help.

But despite his Tourette's, as a child Brad chose to be happy.

"I realized early on that no one wants to hear that you are having a bad day," he said. "And I found that if I tell someone I am having a good day, then all of a sudden my day just got a little bit better. I don't view life as a cup that is half-empty or half-full. I view life as if my cup were over-flowing every day."

Brad learned that thinking positive thoughts and verbalizing those thoughts to others improves his day. He also made a conscious choice to focus not on the few activities that he couldn't do, but on all the great things he could do.

For me, there is no happier visual than to watch a child on a swing. The sheer exuberance of the wind in the child's hair, the huge grin, the complete abandonment of everything in life except that specific moment is something most adults lose somewhere along the way. We've forgotten how to enjoy the moment.

I often see kids skipping through the mall, holding on tightly to the hand of a parent. How many adults do you find skipping along with them? Not many, and that's a shame. Adults don't skip because skipping is considered to be childish and "silly." The reality is that it's great exercise and it's fun. The simple act of skipping makes me happy—which brings me to my point. If you break it down, most of our happiness is not about earning a bazillion dollars or becoming president of our company. Those are certainly great achievements and should definitely be celebrated, but true happiness is found in life's little moments.

Happiness is a special moment with our loved ones; it's a great cup of coffee, a sunny day, a thunderstorm, a good book, a great ball game, or finding a forgotten dollar in a coat pocket. It's the smile of a child, letting a young mother in line ahead of you, finding the perfect chair at a yard sale. Happiness is all around us. Every day brings thousands of opportunities for happiness, but in our hurry and haste to get to the next part of our day, we ignore 99 percent of the happiness that comes our way. The sad fact is that we totally disregard most of our own happiness.

When my son was a year old I found myself a single parent living in a house out in the country with a leaky roof, no water or heat, and plastic covering the windows instead of glass. At night, my son and I would make a game of gathering sticks in the nearby woods to burn in the fireplace. It was our only heat and while not brutal, Tennessee nights can be bitterly cold. I'd make a tent out of the couch, coffee table and some blankets and we'd snuggle up there in front of the fire. I actually slept fairly well during those times because I was happy.

How, you ask, could I be happy when I was living in such dismal circumstances? Well, I had a job I liked. It didn't pay well, but they allowed me flextime whenever my son was ill or I couldn't find a baby sitter, and I liked the people I worked with. I was out in the country with the birds, and trees, and a beautiful river bordering the property. My son was learning about nature, and I had many good friends. Sure, there were a lot of bad events happening in my life during that time, but as a survival method, I chose to be happy.

Of course, I didn't want to stay in those circumstances forever and was making strides to pull out of that situation, but while I was there I, like Brad, chose not to focus on what I didn't have, but to find what positives I could and enjoy them. That enjoyment quickly turned into true happiness.

My situation is not unique. University of Illinois psychologist Ed Diener confirmed in a recent *USA Today* article that, "Materialism is toxic for happiness." *USA Today* went on to report that, "the happiest people surround themselves with family and friends, [and] don't care about keeping up with the Joneses next door. Even rich materialists aren't as happy as those who care less about getting and spending."

Is it wrong to have money and nice clothes? Of course not. We all would like to have enough to live our lives the way we want to without worrying. Does this mean that those who have more resources cannot be happy? Not at all, for it is not what you have that brings true happiness, it is what you do with what you have that matters. Just remember that the happiest people judge themselves by their own yardsticks, never against what others do or have.

No matter how happy you already are, you can always find more enjoyment if you make an effort. Just try a few of the steps below.

Step 1: Do Something Fun and Silly

Do something fun and silly every day this week. My friend Brad Cohen often wears fun hats like those worn by the Cat in the Hat. If you are very conservative in attire, be daring and break up your wardrobe with an unusual pair of socks or a fun tie. If yours is a more colorful style of personality, skip to the lunchroom, do a cartwheel at the bus stop or carry a balloon with you all day, just because you can. You could sing joyously on a street corner, stand in a parking lot and paint a picture, or climb a tree. Now if you haven't done a cartwheel in thirty years, you might want to work into it. You don't want to physically injure yourself. Be reasonable and start with something a little more doable, like a somersault!

Do the things you have always wanted to do but didn't because "real people don't act like that." Forget convention. There is fun in other people's reaction to your silliness—and their reactions are guaranteed to give you something to talk about in your old age. Additionally, you will bring a smile to the faces of everyone who sees you. Every day, choose something new that you think will bring you delight. Take some friends along for the ride and be sure to stop and savor the moment. You will want to record your choice of activities in your *Success Within* notebook and also record the varied responses of those around you.

Step 2: Stop Worrying About What You Don't Have

Stop worrying about what your neighbors and friends have that you don't, and make a list of all the wonderful belongings you do have that bring you happiness—not what you are grateful for or need, but things that make you happy. Your list might include your children, a hummingbird who visits in the morning, a special friend, hot chocolate, rollerskating, or blueberries. There are no right or wrong answers, but it is important to identify what simple items and activities bring you joy so you can focus on them, rather than the negative areas of your life.

Step 3: Choose to be Happy

Choose to be happy. There is good in all situations, it is just up to you to find it. By focusing on the positive elements of a situation rather than the negative, you will find yourself a happier person. Of course, you can't ignore the negative; you just have to find a positive way to think about it.

For example, I was once flying to a performance with a client and his band. We were all a little irked that who ever booked the tickets had chosen a route that included two very lengthy layovers when there had been several direct flights. But instead of being upset over a situation that we could do nothing about, my client chose to have fun. How can you have fun in an airport? By standing in the center of a busy hallway and pretending to be Elvis. My client strummed his air guitar for all he was worth and sang several popular Elvis tunes. The look on people's faces as they passed was priceless. My client brightened their day as much as he did ours—and his own. Instead of sitting in a boring airport griping about the delay, we all had a great time. It's a wonderful memory I will carry with me forever.

Last week in Step 4, you chose the one item from each day that you needed. Every day this week, review your entire day and choose the one event that made you the happiest—your happiest single moment from the many moments in your day. After a while you will begin seeing a theme to your own happiness and it will become something you can draw from when you are down.

Week 5 Success Plan

* Choose to be happy
* Do something silly every day
* Make a list of the things that bring you happiness
* Choose your happiest moment of the day

Week 6

BEING THE BEST

"Acquire peace of mind by becoming the best you are capable of being." —Coach John Wooden

When I was very young, a woman named Katherine Moline came once or twice a week to clean our house. Sometimes when she was there, we had lunch together at an old table downstairs that overlooked the garden and the lake. During one pre-kindergarten conversation when we were talking about whether I should be a truck driver or a veterinarian when I grew up, Mrs. Moline passed along something her father once told her that I have never forgotten. "There's no shame in cleaning other people's houses, or in any occupation," he said, "as long as you are the best house cleaner, or the best whatever, that you can possibly be."

As I grew up, that thought was always in the back of my mind, but it jumped to the forefront when I heard it again some ten years later. When I was about fifteen I had a riding instructor who changed my life. Ironically, he most likely never knew what a major impact a few little words had on me. I had just started showing horses and, after some initial success followed by a major growth spurt, I was floundering. I went to the instructor for help, obsessed with the idea of beating the three or four people who consistently placed above me.

But he had other ideas. He told me to forget about others and concentrate on myself. "Be the best *you* that you can be," he said, "and the rest will fall in place."

Be the best *you* that you can be. It really is a very simple concept. It was also something I could relate to because my ultimate goal, you see, was not to beat the other people, but to win the class—and there is a huge difference in those two concepts. Focusing on beating someone else wastes time and energy because it does nothing to improve your skills or who you are as a person. By focusing on yourself, you are spending time and energy positively, improving your abilities and growing as a person.

Once I began looking at my goal from a different angle, I found there was another way to reach it. I did not have to "beat" another competitor in order to win; I could "earn" the win by being the best I could be.

As soon as I put that principle into place, I almost immediately began placing ahead of some of the people I once wanted to beat. Before too long, I was at the top of the class as often as they were and I knew I had achieved my goal. And throughout my life, I have taken the concept of being the best *you* that you can be into everything I do.

The concept of "beating" someone else begins very early in all of our lives. Even toddlers are encouraged to be the fastest or the best. Kids are encouraged to win at all costs, rather than encouraged to become more skilled. Once a child starts school, the trend continues when they are urged to beat Josh in spelling, or Katie on the soccer field. It doesn't matter that Katie is an athletic wonder and beating her is next to impossible. Instead of feeling pumped because a child had a much better practice than the day before, a child comes away discouraged because she still didn't "beat" the star athlete. In her eyes, she lost, when in fact she should be celebrating her improved abilities.

Wanting to do better than another is a normal, human feeling. But focusing on beating another defeats the purpose. The only way to pass Josh in spelling is to work hard and concentrate on your own spelling skills. By concentrating on yourself, you'll end up far ahead of Josh, and all the other spellers as well, not because you beat him, but because through hard work you have become a wonderful speller.

Competition is good for us all, but it should be used as a test of abilities rather than as a measuring stick for self-worth. Instead of being taught to beat the other kid, a child should learn that it is important to do a better job individually than he did the last time. He needs to learn specific steps to improve his own efforts. What can he do as an individual to be better at this particular task than he was the last time around?

We also need to recognize that every person has different strengths and weaknesses. James might climb trees better than Sarah, but Sarah is a better swimmer. Does the fact that James does a better job in the tree department make him a better person? Of course not. When you are a kid, the skills are equally important, but different, so you cannot compare. Is the person in the next cubicle a better employee because he types faster than you do? Not necessarily. You might be a better people person. Which is more important depends on the job and the needs of the organization. Can you compare the effort a paraplegic athlete makes in a 5k race versus that of an able bodied athlete in a marathon? Not at all. In short, you cannot worry about other people or compare yourself to them. You only can focus on you and take action to do a better job in all the different areas of your life.

The concept of being the best *you* that you can be is used by many sports coaches, most notably former UCLA basketball coach John Wooden who, instead of encouraging his players to beat the other team, motivated his athletes to "outscore" the opponent through relentless drills, fundamental work and conditioning. His concept worked incredibly well as he won the NCAA basketball championship an unprecedented ten out of twelve consecutive years. More importantly, virtually all of his players went on to excel in their chosen careers because they had learned to focus on being the best they could be, and knew how to apply it to all areas of their life.

In addition to our individual strengths and weaknesses, and our varying levels of abilities and skills, each one of us also has our own set of unique circumstances that we deal with every day. You may have gotten caught in traffic and been late for work, or had to wait for a repairman who never showed up. Your daughter may have picked a fight or the dog had to go to the vet. You might be a fabulous parent, but have a very challenging child, and maybe you put far more effort into parenting than your neighbor does with less than spectacular results. So who is the better parent, you or your neighbor? Again, you cannot compare. Every day we have our own set of individual circumstances that are uniquely ours to deal with.

Step 1: Look in the Mirror Every Night

The success plan for this week is simple. Look in the mirror each night and ask if you were the best *you* that you could have been that day. With the unique set of circumstances you encountered on this given day, did you do the best you were capable of doing? Were you the best Mom you could be? If not, what could you have done differently or better? Were you the best friend, neighbor, employer, or son that you could have been? What unique circumstances fell along your path that helped or hindered you in your efforts?

If you feel you did exceptionally well in any area of your life, give yourself a pat on the back. That's wonderful! If you find there is room for improvement, be easy on yourself. Learn from the situation and make a commitment to do better the next time.

Only you know how well you did or did not do, so be honest, but not too hard on yourself. Yes, you should have opened the door for the older lady and you should have planned extra time to pick your son up at school. But you did a great job handling the staff meeting and were a good ear for your sister.

The first day, give yourself a mental rating then work toward continually raising the bar in every area of your life. If you had an exceptionally fabulous day parenting, celebrate! But work toward having an even better day in that area tomorrow. If you didn't do very well, determine the circumstances that both helped and hindered you, and figure out a way to improve should the situation arise again. You will have ups and downs. That is part of life. But, if you take five minutes every evening to review your day, you will, over time, see major improvements in your relationships, your career, and your ability to plan. The many diverse areas of your life will become much more rewarding because you are actively taking the time to improve them.

Week 6 Success Plan

* Be the best you that you can be every day in all areas of your life
* Look yourself in the mirror each night and analyze your day
* Identify unusual circumstances you dealt with
* Discover the areas in your life in which you need to improve
* Commit to being even better tomorrow

Week 7

LAUGHTER MAKES
THE WORLD GO ROUND

"The most wasted of all days is one without laughter."
—e. e. cummings

Many people have seen the old *Mary Tyler Moore* episode where Chuckles the Clown dies. At the very staid and proper funeral, Mary unsuccessfully tries to hold back the giggles. Before too long she is laughing for all she is worth, and so are the rest of the mourners. It is a very funny episode, and shows how Mary's untimely chortles turned a very sad event into one of shared remembrances and mutual joy in celebrating the life of a loved one.

Can you imagine breaking out in a huge belly laugh in the middle of a funeral? How embarrassing! But as unconventional as Mary's burst of laughter was, it made everyone feel a lot better, and that is not unusual. It has been medically proven that laughter helps us get through difficult times. Numerous research studies have proven that laughter helps people tolerate pain. In one study, researchers at a pain lab at UCLA Medical Center asked healthy children to put their hands in ice-cold water. Watching humorous videos that ranged from old Marx Brothers' films to *The Simpsons* helped the kids endure the ice bath as much as 40 percent longer.

Researchers hope that laughter ultimately will help ease pain in people who have debilitating injuries and diseases. The idea that humor might aid in healing is also gaining respect, even though the general notion that entertainment may be healing is actually very old. Ancient Greeks were known for building hospitals next to amphitheaters for the benefit of their patients. More recently, a Japanese study published in 2001 in the *Journal of the American Medical Association* found that skin welts shrank in allergy patients who watched Charlie Chaplin's comedic classic, *Modern Times*.

Like Mary's laughter at Chuckle's funeral, some of our best laughs come at the most unlikely of times. A few years ago I had Christian singer/songwriter Paul Overstreet doing interviews at country music's main fan-based event, Fan Fair. For many years this event was held at the fairgrounds in Nashville, but was eventually moved to a downtown location. The first year Fan Fair was downtown was quite chaotic. More than twenty thousand musical artists, soap and sports stars, fan club presidents, publicists, media and fans had been in the old location for many years, so finding our way around after the move was "interesting" to say the least.

Well before the event, many publicists (including myself) realized that there was not enough space allocated for artists and media to get together for interviews. Fortunately, some of the merchants on Nashville's lower Broadway— where many small nightclubs are located—jumped in to help by donating extra office space.

At nine o'clock one wet June morning, Paul and I dodged through a thunderstorm and dashed in the back door of the historic Tootsie's Orchid Lounge. This club is located across the alley from the legendary Ryman Auditorium where the long-running radio show, the *Grand Ole Opry* had been aired prior to the move across town to the new "Opry" house in the seventies.

Even though it was early, the place was packed. Paul and I wove our way through one beer drinker after the next, heading toward the staircase at the front of the building that would lead us to private offices upstairs where Paul had interviews scheduled. As we passed the bar, Paul gave a wave to his friend, country artist David Frizzell, who was on Tootsie's tiny stage performing some of his many hits.

When we finally arrived upstairs and had a moment to wipe the rain off, it was time to jump into the first interview. The interview was with a new Christian-based television program that wanted to talk to Paul about how he juggled his strong Christian faith in the country music industry.

As they hit the lights, cued the camera, and began the interview, we suddenly heard through the old floorboards the packed crowd singing enthusiastically along to one of David's more popular songs:

She said: I'm gonna' hire a wino to decorate our home,
So you'll feel more at ease here, and you won't have to roam.
We'll take out the dining room table, and put a bar along that wall,
And a neon sign, to point the way, to our bathroom down the hall.

As the crowd below was singing quite boisterously, our soundman hollered cut, and everything was set up again. Paul and the reporter just looked at each other and smiled and shrugged. As they began the second take, Paul was describing how important his Christianity was to him, David and his crowd wound their way around to the chorus again.

She said: I'm gonna' hire a wino to decorate our home . . .

This time Paul looked helplessly at me and began to chuckle before anyone called "cut." The thought of that particular song being sung so enthusiastically during this particular interview was, in fact, quite funny. This time we all waited until we could hear that the song was finished before beginning take three.

The cameraman finally called "Roll" and the interview began for the third time when we heard a voice bellow from below, "One more time!"

She said: I'm gonna' hire a wino to decorate our home . . .

Paul began to laugh so hard that tears were running down his face. The soundman fell over on the floor, and the reporter had his head back against the wall and was just howling. Fortunately, by the time we were all done laughing, David was done singing, so the interview was finally able to proceed.

It isn't often that you get as good or as long a laugh as we had that day, and that's a shame. In addition to being fun, it is great exercise and usually provides some wonderful moments for us to remember. Too many of us have forgotten the importance of laughing regularly and need to rediscover funny or humorous moments. Sometimes you come across a humorous moment but are so wrapped up in your life that you don't think you have the time to stop and appreciate it. Or worse yet, you don't even recognize the moment. Other times life gets so tough that the only appropriate response is to laugh, and trudge on.

One of the most "successful" people I ever met was an older gentleman named Mr. Gibb. I met him when his wife babysat for my young son. He and his wife had raised seven productive children on a farmer's small income, and had foster parented a number of other children. At the time I knew him, he was looking forward to the birth of his fortieth grandchild and his tenth great-grandchild. When he said he was related to half the people in the county, he meant it! Mr. Gibb's favorite pastime was to sit on his front porch in the evening and tell the tallest tale he could think up. Friends, neighbors, kids and grandkids alike would show up year round after their evening meal and listen to Mr. Gibb, as he described it, "tell lies." Everyone laughed through the evening.

Of all the good qualities about this man, I best remember his face. It was wreathed in laugh lines and was one of the friendliest faces I have ever seen. Without ever being told, Mr. Gibb instinctively knew the power of laughter. He lived in good health well into his nineties, and attributed his longevity to "one good belly laugh a day." I hope some day my face looks just like his.

Step 1: Make Someone Laugh

The first objective this week is to make at least one person laugh every day. Usually, throughout the course of your day, you will come across someone who is a little down. Take a moment to cheer up that person by helping him find the brighter side of life, or by telling a funny story. If you are not used to doing this kind of thing, you may not succeed at first, but by the end of the week, you should have enjoyed making a few people laugh.

Step 2: Look on the Bright Side

Every day you have humorous and not-so-humorous situations happening all around you. This week take the time to acknowledge these situations with laughter. Maybe the copier and your printer both go down on the same day. Instead of getting frazzled and possibly throwing a temper tantrum, laugh. At least your computer still works. Maybe your coat got stuck in the doorway. Instead of impatiently pulling free, do a little dance, make a funny face, enjoy the moment.

Step 3: Find Your Funny Bone

Take time to recall your all-time funniest moment. Throughout all your funny memories, what is the one absolutely funniest moment that you ever experienced? What is the one event that made you laugh harder than anything else? Maybe it was a movie. The grocery store scene with Tim Conway and the mule in *Gus* always gets me rolling. Watching my friend Claudia getting her belt buckle stuck on the gutter and hanging over our college counselor's dorm room window when we were "decorating" the campus at midnight for Halloween is another of my more memorable funny moments. Of course, Claudia may view that a little differently. Schedule some time to talk to your friends and relatives to stir up some of these great memories—I'll bet you can't choose just one!

* Recognize moments each day that are worthy of laughter
* Embrace the "laugh lines" in your face and in those around you
* Make a point to make someone else laugh every day
* Laugh at both your humorous and not-so-humorous moments
* Recall your all-time funniest moment

OPPORTUNITY KNOCKS

"In the middle of every difficulty lies opportunity."
—Albert Einstein

Opportunity knocks, but it doesn't always make noise. Each new day presents you with a host of opportunities, but you have to be aware they exist before you can take advantage of them. You have to be alert enough to realize they are there.

How many times have you wished that you had said or done something—or gone somewhere—and instead you just sat at home? Maybe you were tired, or too busy, or you just did not want to extend the effort to go or do. You may also have passed up an opportunity to learn something new, only to regret it later. Whether it is a skill or new information, you never know when it will come in handy, either then, or later in life.

I find it so exciting that every person you come in contact with every day gives you an opportunity. It is then up to you whether you explore that opportunity or not. It doesn't matter if you are a stay-at-home mom, a corporate CEO, or if you are a person who is retired. Everyone you come into contact with either in person, over the phone, through the mail, or across the Internet, has something to offer you.

I have always made it a point to get to know as many people as I can. I do this not only because I really like people and find everyone I meet fascinating, but because I know that just about everyone at some point will have something to share with me, something that I can learn from, or some way to help me. I now have such a network of friends and acquaintances that I can direct people I know to sources for everything from adult care givers, to strategic analysts. I may not know a specific person who can help, but I probably have a friend or acquaintance who does.

Shortly after I moved to Nashville, I got to know an intern at a newspaper where I was freelancing. She was going to graduate school and was having boyfriend troubles, and when I'd stop by in the evening to file my stories, we'd talk about school and men, grammar and computers, and just about everything else under the sun. Beverly went back to school and we lost touch, then she resurfaced at the same newspaper as a reporter. After a few years she moved into a key position in public relations at a major record label, and now teaches at a local university. She also freelances for several national magazines. Over the years, Beverly Keel has been a wonderful resource for me time and time again, and it all started when she was a lovelorn intern.

Many people have told me that they would have ignored the lowly intern, and instead focused on impressing the boss. If they had, they would have missed a tremendous opportunity to get to know someone who down the line was going to accomplish greatness. You have to learn to look beyond the position and see the person. Everyone has something to offer.

Think of all the places you go during the day, all the people you meet and talk with. You might just go to the store and the post office, but everyone there has an opportunity for you. Maybe it is only the opportunity share a smile and make a sad-faced person feel good about himself, or maybe it is a chance conversation you strike while waiting in line. You might compliment a young girl on what she is wearing and find that her mother is just the baby sitter you have been looking for. If you are job-hunting, maybe the man you meet in the cereal aisle has a position open in his company. It is all a matter of acting on the many opportunities that come to you each day.

My first job in Nashville was as a receptionist at a disc-mastering studio. This was way back when they were still actually making vinyl records. My boss became friends with a booking agent next door and when they went to lunch together, the agent, Eddie Rhines, often ran his phone out on a long cord so I could answer his calls while he was away. At that time, Eddie was handling such acts at Jerry Lee Lewis, Johnny PayCheck, David Allan Coe, and Ricky Nelson, and his phone was quite busy.

After a few months, I left that job and went on to several others, both in and out of the music industry. But Eddie and I stayed in touch. Eventually, I made the decision to open my own business doing graphic design and freelance writing, and sub-leased office space on Nashville's Music Row. As was our custom, I bumped into Eddie at an industry event and told him about my new business.

Not long after that, Eddie gave me a call. Johnny PayCheck was looking for a new publicist and Eddie thought I'd be perfect for the job. Now, I had never done public relations before. I had never taken any PR classes in school, but as Eddie pointed out, I was a journalist. I went to all the music industry events and I knew the key people. My lack of experience made me hesitate in taking the gig, but then I remembered something a college advisor once told me: If you miss an opportunity to move up the ladder, you will never know whether or not you could have handled the job.

I took PayCheck on as a client and within three months, I was well into what would be an almost twenty year career as an entertainment publicist. A casual introduction from my former boss had given me an entirely new career. Opportunity does knock. Are you listening?

Step 1: Recognize Opportunity

This week it is especially important to understand that every day you meet at least one person who has an opportunity for you. The opportunity could be as simple as you opening the door for a child—thus making you feel good while making their life a little easier—or it could be the chance to make a new friend, find employment, join a club, or take a trip. Many opportunities are limited in time and scope; they are small opportunities. Others, like my meeting Eddie Rhines, can be life changing.

Keep a running list this week of all the opportunities that come your way, large or small. Your list might include:

* Said hi to the neighbors and learned they are looking for a used refrigerator. Hope to sell them ours.
* Met a guy at the store who backpacks and who gave me ideas on some great places to go.
* Helped an older couple carry groceries. Learned they live near my son and could water his plants when he is traveling.

By the end of the week you will be an expert at recognizing new opportunities and be amazed at what life really has to offer.

Step 2: Create Your Own Adventure Day Opportunity
In addition to recognizing the opportunities that fall your way, this week you will create some of your own opportunities through an adventure day. Your adventure day might be a few hours long, or it might consist of an entire weekend. The challenge in an adventure day is to go somewhere or do something you have never done before. You can do it alone or with a neighbor or friends or family—whatever you choose. You might pick a town on the map that is an hour or so drive from your home. Hopefully, you will have never been to the town before and will have time to meet some of the people there and explore. If transportation is a problem, take the bus to a part of town you have never been to, or walk to a different part of your neighborhood. If time is of the essence, take an afternoon or evening and visit a store or a park you have not been to before.

You might also try a new activity. If you've always wanted to learn woodworking, or to play the guitar, take a class. Many towns offer free adult education classes through their high school, parks, or community colleges. Churches also sometimes offer free classes. Experience the new activity and meet the people who are involved. You never know whom you will meet or what hidden talent you might discover.

The idea is to discover all the opportunities the area or activity has to offer. Look at the people, the buildings, the trees, the wildlife. Meet the people. Take time to observe.

Read the local literature, whether it is a newspaper or a park brochure. Talk to whomever serves you lunch, or the couple you meet on the walking trail.

The fun is in the unexpected. You never know what you will see. And, you could quite possibly experience several of your greatest moments.

Week 8 Success Plan

* Recognize that opportunity is all around you
* Keep a daily list of your opportunities, large and small
* Plan and carry out an adventure day opportunity

GREAT, YOU MADE A MISTAKE!

"The only real mistake is the one from which we learn nothing."
—John Powell

When I was showing horses, I once lost the possibility of a national driving championship when one side of the cart became separated from the horse due to a faulty latch. The cart I was driving attached to the horse's harness by a cross bar in front the of the cart and two "side poles," each running on one side of the horse. Each side pole attached to one end of the crossbar with a latch. In the middle of the class I looked down to find one of the side poles had separated from the cross bar. I reached down to try to reattach the side pole to the cart, and in the process not only put myself in danger, but also everyone else in the class. I was especially upset because the entire situation was my fault; the same exact episode had happened a month or so before during a training session. While it had happened only the one time, I knew the latch needed to be replaced and I didn't do anything about it. Since that time, I have been meticulous about checking my equipment—everything from shoelaces to computers to tires.

I don't know if I would have won that championship, but I do know that until the latch slipped we were having a really good class, and I think our entry would have been in the top placings. But while I was terribly disappointed in myself at the time, I learned several lessons:

* Double check your equipment
* If you know something needs to be done, do it
* Learn from your mistake and move on

Time is wonderful in that it lends perspective. Today, I appreciate far more the lessons I learned from that experience than any championship I could have won.

Everyone makes mistakes and that's good, because contrary to popular opinion, mistakes are good. Each mistake you make is wonderful because it is a learning opportunity. From the stereotypical child who puts her hand on a hot stove, to treating another person unfairly, or forgetting to do something, mistakes are made every day. The mistake itself is not important; but what you do with the mistake is.

Mistakes are a great opportunity for personal growth. If, for example, you forget to lock your door and a thief comes in and makes off with your new large screen TV, you are going to remember to lock your door. It's an expensive lesson, but those are the ones you learn from most. Long term, if you learn from the lesson and don't repeat the action, the mistake was usually worth it.

In addition to recognizing the action—or lack thereof—that caused the mistake, you also have to take responsibility for your mistakes. This means you need to do whatever possible to right the mistake without causing further damage. You need to examine the mistake, understand why it happened, and learn from the error so it does not happen again. Some people continue to make the same mistakes over and over. (Your daughter might get stuck in a repetitive cycle she has not taken the time to really look at her mistakes and learn from them.)

I have always driven a pick-up truck, partially so I could save on moving costs when I moved, which used to be frequently, but also so I could help friends move. At first I'd load up the truck with as much heavy furniture as I could load onto the bed. But it only took one experience for me to realize that, with all the weight in the back of the truck, when one of the rear truck tires goes flat, it doesn't take too long for the other one to follow. Ten hours spent in the Arizona desert with only one spare tire when I needed two ensured from that point on I always carried several spares. I also learned the importance of following up with written thank-you's and a small gift to those who go out of their way to help you. It isn't often that people stop to help a stranger; they need to know how much they are appreciated.

When my purse—which was in plain sight in a locked hotel room—was stolen, I learned never to leave my purse lying around anywhere, even if the room was locked. That little blunder ensured that my employees did not get their per diem that day, so if it had not been for the generosity of others, who pitched in until my bank could wire additional funds, my staff would not have eaten. I hope I made my apologies clear to each and every one of them.

When I was a publicist for Johnny PayCheck, I knew he was not a good driver. He often was on his bus or in the company of one of his band members and did not have much opportunity to drive, so he didn't get much practice. I knew this and yet when John and I left a Nashville-area studio late one night I let him drive. John alternately—and for no apparent reason—put his foot on the gas or the brake as we made our way jerkingly down the road toward the freeway, and when he turned the wrong way onto an exit instead of an entrance ramp, the swarm of lights suddenly headed our way made me realize letting John drive had been a huge mistake. Fortunately, he realized it, too, and after backing down the exit ramp and enduring a blare of honking horns, we switched places.

I didn't want John to get mad at me—I was the publicist and he was the artist, so in a way we were in an employer/employee situation. I also didn't want to hurt his feelings or tear down his confidence by suggesting the change in drivers. So in several ways it would have been very easy for me to sit tight with this legendary client and let him try to bring us home safely. But after the ramp incident I knew I had to make a change in the driving situation and Johnny knew it, too. "Everyone," he said philosophically after he was settled comfortably in the passenger seat, "can't be good at everything." I can't say that John never drove at night after that, but I know I never again rode with him when he was driving! We both knew how fortunate we were that no one was hurt.

In each of these situations, a mistake was made and a lesson was learned. I cherish each of these experiences, for as difficult as they were at the time, going through each experience and learning from it has made my life since then a little bit easier.

Step 1: Identify Your Mistakes
This week it is time to sit in quiet reflection and identify five to seven major mistakes you have made in your life. One might be a former spouse whom you didn't treat as well as you should have, or an error you made at work that cost

you your job. Just go back in your life and identify a handful of your biggest mistakes. This exercise is not designed to induce guilt or to become depressed over a "what could have been." Rather, it is meant to be a celebration of your growth as an individual and the lessons you have learned. Additionally, the more we evaluate our past mistakes, the less likely we are to make a similar mistake in our future.

Step 2: Analyze the Blunder

Think about each instance and remember what the circumstances were in your life that led to the slip-up. You might want to discuss this with family or friends who knew you at the time, and get their perspective. Maybe you were overworked, or stressed with personal issues so you weren't making good judgments. You could have been strapped for cash, or worried about a child. Possibly you were just naive. I did a lot of things when I was younger that I shouldn't have, and the only reason I can find was that I was "young and dumb."

Step 3: Find the Lesson

Then, with the perspective of time, discover what the experience taught you. If you treated a former spouse poorly, did the lesson you learned help in relationships after that? If you slacked off at work and were fired because of it, are you now more focused in your work environment? Know that every mistake offers some sort of learning experience. If you can't find a way the blunder improved your future, consider what lessons the mistake offered. Is there a lesson to be learned that you have missed?

Step 4: Forgive Yourself

There should be some good in every one of these major blunders in your life. And in that goodness, you should be able to forgive yourself. Maybe your job loss threw your family into bankruptcy. But did it also pull you closer together? Did you find less expensive activities you could enjoy? Are you happier now in your work situation than you were in your old? Maybe it made your kids appreciate money more? It could have made your sons more frugal, or more accountable to their spending habits. If you can find the lesson, you should be able to forgive yourself. You are, after all, only human. Allow yourself the blessing of forgiveness.

Step 5: Move On

Once you've identified and analyzed the major mistakes in your life, move on with a renewed commitment to avoid making that same mistake again.

Week 9 Success Plan

* Recognize that we all make mistakes
* Mistakes don't matter, what you learn from them does
* Identify the major mistakes in your life
* Analyze how and why they occurred
* Find the lesson in the mistake
* Forgive yourself
* Move on

Week 10

HARD TIMES AHEAD

"Yesterday I dared to struggle. Today I dare to win."
—Bernadette Devlin

While we all hope we will sail through life without any hardship, the reality is that just about everyone will face some tough obstacles. Sometimes it seems we are given more than we can stand, but one way or another we always pull through. This week is all about handling tough times with style and grace.

When my son was three, I decided to open my own business. My last day of work at my old job, his babysitter called and said Colby was sick. She suggested I take him to the doctor right away. By the time I had wrapped up a few instructions for my successor and cleaned out my desk, an hour had passed and she had called twice more.

The babysitter and I both thought Colby was coming down with a severe upper respiratory infection—something he had been susceptible to since birth. But when I met with the pediatrician, I learned Colby was having his first asthma episode and he was immediately admitted to a local hospital where we spent the next five days.

It's always difficult when you have a child who is ill. You suddenly are dealing with issues you are not prepared to deal with. The animals at home need to be fed, and you have no change of clothes. You didn't bring any money for food. Additionally, you are terrified for your child, and don't sleep much—if at all. Very quickly you become exhausted both mentally and physically.

I had no family in the area who could help during this time, but I was fortunate in that a neighbor was able to take care of the small menagerie we had at home. And so I could eat, a friend loaned me a few dollars until I could get to the bank to cash a check. (This was long before the days of ATMs on every corner.)

On our second day at the hospital, I signed the papers for my business loan and computer lease while sitting by my son's bed. On the third day the hospital found a volunteer to stay with Colby while I went home to change clothes, shower, check the mail, and cash a check. I had also developed a sinus infection and needed to pick up some antihistamines. When I arrived home, I found that the electricity had been turned off. I had planned on running a check by the electric company the day Colby got sick; with all that was going on I had forgotten about it. I did a quick cold-water sponge bath and was so emotionally drained by the time I climbed back into my car that I barely had enough energy to drive back to the hospital.

After I parked the car in the hospital parking lot, I slipped on a patch of oil and broke my foot. I clearly re-member lying there flat on my back in the middle of the parking garage with tears streaming down my face, not really caring if I got run over or not. It obviously was not my time, for no car came along to oblige me in my wishes. Eventually I got up and limped back up to Colby's room to relieve the volunteer sitter. I knew my foot was broken, and even though I was in a hospital, I didn't have anyone to stay with Colby while I went to the emergency room. My foot could wait. I spent that night and the next day and night in a chair next to Colby's bed with my foot propped on a stool.

When it was time for Colby to be discharged on the fifth day, I finally went to the emergency room where a resident doctor pronounced my foot officially broken, wrapped it up and sent us home.

I mention all of this not because I want to wallow in the misery of that time, but because even though I was going through a very difficult period, I was extremely grateful. The child in the bed next to Colby was there for "failure to thrive." He was almost three, looked not much more than one and was fed through a tube in his stomach. There were children in the hospital playroom who had lost limbs to cancer, and others in wheelchairs who would never walk.

Somehow, all of these children and their families remained upbeat, and I knew as hard a time as I was having, it was nothing compared to what these extraordinary people were dealing with. All of them were handling their own tragic situations with supreme grace and humility; they definitely were not lying on a garage floor, totally overwhelmed with life, hoping to be run over. There's an old proverb that states if given the chance to walk in someone else's shoes, you'll want your own shoes back, and that was very true here.

So when I limped out of the hospital with my sinus infection and my child—who would have trouble breathing for many years to come—and headed to a home with no power or lights, I was very, very happy. I was appreciative that my child had asthma, because it could have been something much, much worse. I was grateful I had a home to go to, for there were many homeless people who did not. I was thrilled I had only broken my foot and not my back or my neck.

Those few days in the hospital had given me some time to think, and I realized how much I had learned by watching those courageous kids and their families. Those who were coping the best were the ones who were very focused on a goal of regaining their health. These people were also very involved in helping those around them. The kids with the miraculous rebounds were the ones who were helping the weaker ones move down the hallways. They were the ones with the smiles on their faces while they determinedly fought back.

I learned a great deal in those few days about the steps involved in facing adversity. Tough times build strength, and the more you're given, the more you develop and grow. This week you will learn to handle your own tough times as well as those of others.

Step 1: Find Someone to Help
Hard times are relative. What may be life shattering to one, is of no consequence to another. A teen may be crushed because she was snubbed at school; a man may have lost a parent in a car accident. Each of them is going through a hard time—one problem is perceived and the other is real—but each in its own way is distressing for that person. Your job this week is to help one person in your inner circle who has a problem, using the steps outlined below. This person could be you. It could be a family member, a friend, a neighbor, or a co-worker.

Step 2: Breathe
Hard times usually do not go away by themselves. You have to work at pushing them out of your life and the first

step, whether you are helping yourself or someone else, is to take a deep breath and clear your mind. Breathe deeply and quietly for as long and as often as it takes for you to focus on a specific troublesome event, rather than the swirl of emotion and confusion that overwhelms you. Once you are calm and focused, you can proceed.

Step 3: Identify and Gather Resources

Everyone has resources, whether they are inner resources of strength and thought, or external resources such as money and friends. When you are—or a someone close to you is—having trouble, thoroughly identify the resources needed to solve the situation then gather them close to you. Find people who know others who can help, and identify the personal strengths you are going to need to work through this time.

Step 4: Find a Strategy and Follow Through

Make a plan, and write it down. Design a plan that will make these hard times go away. If you or a loved one is facing foreclosure on a house, for instance, legal help is needed, as is cash. You probably need a better—or a second—job. You may need financial counseling. Find ways to drum up cash, like a yard sale where you sell everything but the house. If you are ill, find information on your illness, become informed and do whatever it takes to regain your health.

Step 5: Focus on Your Goals

Nothing happens by itself. Make time every day to work on your problem. Be single minded in your efforts, and go all out to make the situation better. To help you focus, also take time to incorporate the visualization skills discussed in Week 1. Visualize the problem going away.

Step 6: Stay Positive

Be grateful for what you do have, because no matter how bad it is, it always can be worse. Listen to motivational or inspirational tapes. Make lists of the good stuff in your life. Pamper yourself with a walk or a bubble bath or some quiet time, and do not allow negative thought in or around you.

Step 7: Help Others

When you need a break from your own troubles, there is nothing to put them in perspective like helping another. The skills you employ in helping another will come in handy with your own problems as well.

Step 8: Smile

Smiling in the face of adversity is a true measure of personal strength. It is a way to gather your inner resources and make headway in the world for one more day. When you smile, you will find people smiling back at you, and all of a sudden your day just became a little bit nicer.

Week 10 Success Plan

* ✱ Find someone you can help
* ✱ Breathe deeply and often to clear your mind
* ✱ Identify your resources
* ✱ Develop a strategy and focus on following through
* ✱ Stay positive
* ✱ Help someone else
* ✱ Smile

DIFFERENT YET THE SAME

*"We all live with the objective of being happy;
our lives are all different and yet the same."*
—Anne Frank

We live in a wide and wonderful world full of many different types of people. Each person has their own history, traditions, political ideas, and religion that make up his or her beliefs. A Jewish girl growing up in Israel is going to have different life experiences than a boy growing up Irish Catholic in Boston. Everything is different: from the schools each attends and the styles of learning those schools adopt, to the different holidays they celebrate, the food they eat, and the sports they watch.

Different does not mean better—or worse. Different does not mean right or wrong. Different just means different. Unfortunately, for thousands of years world governments have gone to war over "different," and—as with the United States Civil War—families have been torn apart again and again over different. Just think what a boring world this would be if we all were exactly the same. What would it be like if we all dressed exactly the same, ate the same foods, participated in the same sports, and were interested in the same things?

My son has a friend who works in a funeral home. "Jonas" has, in fact, just been promoted from gravedigger to the embalming room. Now, I think that would be a terrible job, but Jonas loves it.

I once went out with a dentist. I just can't imagine spending my day with my fingers in other people's mouths, but he was really into it and his eyes lit up as he talked about bicuspids and molars. I love writing and public speaking and find it odd that the thought of either terrifies many others.

The one area we all have in common, though, is that while we are a sum of our experiences, our beliefs are the core of our existence. It's important to stand up for our beliefs, but it is also important to recognize, respect and honor the beliefs of others. When my son was in his early teens he ran away from home. Not once, but numerous times. He, in his infinite wisdom, thought our life at home should be one way, and I in mine thought another. After several harrowing years that included counselors, interventions, soul searching, and group homes, we both finally came to respect each other's ideas. I don't necessarily agree with him all the time, nor he with me. But we each can make legitimate cases for our ideas and can convey to the other why we think the way we do. We often even find ourselves on the same side of an argument even though our reasoning might be poles apart. I have come to respect his ideas and thoughts, and hope he does mine. We are very different, yet we are much the same.

Wouldn't it be an amazing concept if we were able to enjoy each other's diversity and all get along? Of course, that is much easier said than done as we've been fighting almost since time began. The first key to getting along is in understanding other people—and to do that you have to learn about the history, thoughts, ideas and beliefs of people who are different than you.

Step 1: Get to Know "Different" People

This week will be a lot of fun as you talk to people who are different from you. What their differences are is up to you. A co-worker may have a different religion or diverging political views. A neighbor may have grown up in a different country, or come from a small family, while yours was large. Maybe your boss is old and you are young. A teacher might be of a different race. You may have grown up in the city while your spouse is fresh off the farm.

You can easily find people who are different—they are all around you. You work with people, live next door to people, go to church with people, ride the subway with people and are related to people. There are people in the library, the post office, the grocery store, and a host of other places, so you should not have any difficulty in finding people who are different from you. If you are the type who does not get out much, your contact with people may be over the phone, through the mail, or over the Internet. The world is full of unique individuals, if you look, you will find them.

For example, maybe you work with a man you cannot relate with. If you clash regularly with him, ask him to lunch. Just say, "I know we don't get along sometimes, but I'd like to learn more about you so I can understand your views." Most people will take you up on your offer.

Other openers can include: "I know you are a supporter of Cause XYZ, I'd like to know more about that. Do you have time some day soon to tell me about it?" Or, "I understand you were born in Nigeria, I'd love to talk to you someday about what it was like growing up there."

You might ride the bus with a man who dresses in native garb or wears clothing reflecting his faith. Ask him about the significance of his attire. Talk with this new friend and try to understand life from his experience and point of view. If he thinks differently than you do, he may have valid reasons that had not occurred to you.

On the old sitcom, *All in the Family*, Archie Bunker and his son-in-law, Michael, had wildly different views on everything from religion to sports to equal rights. But because Archie and Michael lived in the same house, and because they both loved Archie's daughter, Gloria, they listened to each other's views. Archie and Michael rarely agreed with each other, but they listened. Over time, they even learned to love one another.

If you are non-judgmental and genuinely interested in people, people will talk to you. This week you might talk to one person or to twenty—the more the better!

Step 2: Think

After you've talked with a number of different people, think about each one individually. Did each adequately explain his or her differences to you? If not, what else are you eager to learn? If possible, go back and talk to that person again. Did any of the people you talked with make you think about life differently? Did you understand their point of view better after your discussion with them? Did you find you had anything in common? You may want to discuss your thoughts with those around you and hear what they have to say as well.

There is much to be learned from those who are different, both about your beliefs and those of differing opinions.

Step 3: Learn One Thing

Think about the different people you talked with and what you learned, then choose one thing that meant the most to you. Decide why it was important to you and what difference, if any, it will make in your life.

Week 11 Success Plan

* Understand that we are different, yet the same
* Find as many people as you can who are different from you and talk to them
* Think about what they say and discuss your thoughts with others
* Identify the one thing you learned that meant the most to you

Week 12

RAISING THE BAR

"In these days, a man who says a thing cannot be done is quite apt
to be interrupted by some idiot doing it."
—Elbert Hubbard

No matter where you are or how far you've come, there is always room for improvement. It's easy when there is someone nudging you along the way, but sometimes you have to nudge yourself along.

Chris LeDoux was a world champion bareback rider who went on to make a big name for himself in the music industry. As a teen, he wanted nothing more than to be a rodeo cowboy and began practicing every day after school. His efforts paid off with a few wins at local rodeos, and by the time he was in high school, he was winning at the state level. But Chris knew it wasn't enough. He could be better.

While reading a rodeo magazine, he heard of a rank bucking mare on the world championship rodeo circuit named Necklace, and it became his goal to ride that mare, even though in his wildest dreams he never thought the opportunity would ever arise.

"I can remember any time I'd be out training, running or lifting weights in high school," Chris once told me, "I'd think 'Necklace, Necklace,' and it'd make me run a little faster, run a little harder, lift weights a little heavier, practice on more bales of hay, and work to get a little stronger."

In 1974, Chris finally had the opportunity to ride Necklace, and he said a stick of dynamite could not have blown him off that mare. In Necklace, Chris had found the motivation he needed to become the best he could be.

So what is it that motivates you? Everyone finds their motivation in different ways. Competition might motivate you—or friendship, or learning a new skill. For others, it is being part of a team. For some, a specific goal is motivation.

Helping kids motivates former major league baseball player Jim Eisenreich. A member of the 1997 world champion Florida Marlins, Jim has Tourette Syndrome, which causes vocal and facial twitches and tics. After he retired from the game he could have retired from public life, as many with Tourette's do. But Jim knew how tough it is to live with this disorder and he wanted to help kids with Tourette's live a better life.

So Jim founded the Jim Eisenreich Foundation for Children with Tourette Syndrome and now speaks regularly across the country to children and families affected by Tourette's. Rather than leave it at that, every day Jim asks himself what more he can do. How can he reach more people, perfect his message, change the lives of more children for the better? Jim then uses the success strategies he learned playing professional baseball to push himself to do a better job at what he already does very well, because he knows if he does a better job, he will reach more children and more families, and change more lives. So every day, Jim Eisenreich is out there raising the bar for himself and others.

You are no different than Jim. Every day you are involved in hundreds of activities, and no matter how well you do each of those many things, you can do better. By raising the bar on your performance in everything you do every day, you—like Jim—will touch more people, influence more lives, and achieve greater personal satisfaction. It will also open the door for you in career advancement, pay raises, relationships, and countless other areas that will surprise and amaze you.

What kind of world would this be if we all worked to our fullest potential? What would happen to us individually, as families and as a society? How much could we accomplish if work and family relationships were healthy—if we all pulled together to improve our lives?

On a smaller scale, how would it improve the lives of your children, family and co-workers if you were their role model? Would it help them strive to do better? Would it instill in those close to you the importance of being the best they could possibly be? And if that occurred, what incredible opportunities would then become available to them?

It is pretty unrealistic to think this will all magically happen on its own, but it will never happen on any scale large or small if we each as individuals do not begin somewhere, somehow, to be the best we can be in everything that we do.

Step 1: Analyze Everything You Do This Week

What is the first thing you do when you get up in the morning? You probably put the coffee on and get ready for your day. Have you ever stopped to think how you could make that a more efficient, more pleasurable time? If you awoke five minutes earlier could you spend a few more minutes with your kids? If you left for work five minutes later would you miss some traffic and still arrive on time?

This week involves breaking your day into parts.

What do you do after you've started your day? Do you go to work, work out, clean the house, garden, run errands, play with the grandkids? Once you have identified the various parts of your day, figure out a way to make each part more efficient and more fun. In your *Success Within* journal or notebook, jot down ideas about staying focused when you are with your grandchildren. Compile specific ideas that will help you simplify routine cleaning chores. Make a plan for the errands you need to run, so you are not wasting time by driving back and forth all over town. Map out each section of your day every day in this manner—from house cleaning, to errands, to parenting and relationships, career, to sports and leisure, etc.—and determine how you can be more efficient, do a better job, and have more fun in all that you do.

Step 2: Enlist Aid from Family and Friends

Share your success plan for this week with family or friends. Solicit their help and ideas. Can you teach your seven-year-old daughter to put out her own school clothes the night before? Can a friend try a little harder not to be late for dinner dates? You might be surprised at the innovative ideas your friends and loved ones come up with. Your family might have suggestions about how everyone can work together to help facilitate the laundry process. Co-workers could assist with ideas for streamlining office duties. Who knows, you might come up with some wonderful ideas of your own. More importantly, by raising the bar on your own life, you are pulling those around you up with you.

Once you are able to fine tune one area of your life, you will be surprised at how easily other areas fall together. Suddenly, instead of trying to do one hundred activities all at the same time, you have time and focus to do each individual job better than you have ever done it before.

Step 3: Implement the Ideas
Be sure to implement the new ideas as soon as possible. Some will work, some won't, so you'll probably have to reconvene to tweak the processes. Keep at it until you find a way to make each of the different areas in your life more fun, easier to deal with and less stressful.

Week 12 Success Plan

* Question your performance in all that you do
* Discuss with family and friends ways to improve your, and their, daily activities
* Implement the ideas
* Tweak what isn't working and try again

Week 13

REPEAT

"Any idea, plan, or purpose may be placed in the mind through repetition of thought." —Napoleon Hill

It is thought that the human brain needs thirty days to change, or to create a new habit. Any less time, and you are likely to slip back into your old ways. That's why after each thirteen-week session, you have the opportunity to go back over the previous twelve weeks to reaffirm and re-evaluate some of your new and memorable moments. After this evaluation you may choose to move on to the next thirteen-week section, or if you feel you can benefit, go back and revisit certain weeks.

Step 1: Evaluate

This week is all about evaluation. Find some time this week, either alone or with your *Success Within* partner or group, to think about the following questions. You might want to do this while you are taking a long walk, or while you are spending time with a circle of close friends. Depending on your personality this might be a solitary pursuit or one in which you are accompanied by others. For some, this evaluation process will even create some of its own memorable moments.

You will want to write your answers down for future reference. Some of your answers you might want to discuss with others; some you may wish to keep private. These are *your* memories, *your* moments and *your* choices, and you may be very surprised at what you find!

1. Which week was the easiest for you? The most fun? The toughest? Why?

2. Which week, if any, do you feel you need to revisit? Why?

3. Which week gave you the biggest surprise? In what way?

4. Do you need more time to fully benefit from the success plan of any given week? How will you create that time?

5. Which element of any success plan would you like to keep up with, but have not been able to work into your schedule? What steps can you take to make that a reality?

6. How many memorable moments were you able to create—memories that you will remember forever?

7. Are there any weeks that you did not complete? Why do you think that is?

8. What was the nicest moment of the past twelve weeks? How did it come about?

9. How have these moments changed you?

10. What is one thing you now look at differently?

11. In Week 1, were you able to juggle your daily activities to find a few extra minutes? Did visualizing a goal make it easier for you to reach it?

12. During Week 2, how many dreams, desires and goals were you able to come up with? How many of the individual items on those lists have you completed so far?

13. What great memory did you revisit in Week 3? Were there any memories you have forgotten about that this exercise helped you to remember? Who did you find to revisit memories with? What do you think their reaction was to your memories?

14. How much "stuff" did you weed out in Week 4, and what creative ways did you find to get rid of it? How successful were you at resisting temptation in your purchasing, and how much money did you save? Did you find a theme in your "Daily Picks?"

15. In Week 5, what fun and silly things did you find to do? On the list of things that made you happy each day, were the items similar, or different?

16. In Week 6, how did you fare in being the best *you* that you can be? How did this concept make you aware of your strengths and shortcomings? Have you been able to raise the bar in any areas of your life? If so, which ones?

17. How many people did you make laugh in Week 7 and what did you do to get the laugh? What was your funniest experience?

18. What unique opportunities did you discover in Week 8? Where did you go during your Adventure Day? What new experiences did you have during this exercise?

19. In Week 9, what life mistakes did you identify? What specific things did you learn from these mistakes? Have you made similar errors over and over again? If so, what can you do to get past those mistakes?

20. Who did you find to help in Week 10? What resources

did you have to gather to help them? How did you motivate the person you helped to stay positive?

21. What kinds of "different" people did you find in Week 11? What did you learn from them? Did this exercise change any of your views or beliefs? Did it make you more open to new ideas or thoughts?

22. Did Week 12 help your life to run more smoothly? What one section of your life benefited the most from this assignment?

Week 13 Success Plan

* Evaluate the first twelve weeks
* Take some quiet time to think about answers to the questions listed above

2
TREATING OTHERS WELL

Each week in Part 2 deals with how well you treat other people. Here, you begin to reach out, and by treating others extraordinarily well you will find the extraordinary coming back to you. In the process, you will create some of life's greatest moments. You'll also see another exciting development begin to happen: the knowledge that you are suddenly doing better in many areas of your life. All of a sudden relationships, work life, and home life are coming together as never before. It's a simple thing. It's called success.

Week 14

CHOOSE UP INSTEAD OF DOWN

"I can live for two months on a good compliment."
—Mark Twain

Remember my friend Jennifer from the introduction? She's the one who always has a smile on her face, who always has something nice to say to a stranger. She does it because it makes her feel like a million bucks. Jennifer has found that complimenting others brings her life back into focus and keeps her priorities in order.

Wouldn't it be a wonderful world if everyone were like that—if everyone simply helped each other? What kind of world would it become if everyone complimented each other regularly, if people were actually nice to one another?

This week allows everyone to be the start of something very cool—putting people up. How many times have you been put down? How many negative comments are addressed to you each and every day—by your children, your spouse, your co-workers, and even by strangers? If you are like most people, you get more neutral and negative comments thrown your way than positive ones. This week challenges you to change that trend by complimenting six people every day. Any six people. Or, if you don't come into contact with that many people, you can compliment three people twice, or the same person six times. Handing out six compliments a day will make you feel great, and maybe, just maybe, some of those people will pass a compliment on to someone else.

The idea is to find something you truly like about the person and let him know. If he is a stranger to you, you might compliment his smile, his haircut, or his clothes. If he holds the door for you, say more than just thank you, tell him how much you really appreciated it, and let him know that most people would not have held that door. The fact that he did makes him special. This person who is a stranger to you might think you are a little weird, gushing so about a door, but I guarantee he will not forget you, because he will feel great for the rest of his day.

Instead of a perfunctory thank you, tell the person who bags your groceries how much you value her efforts. Tell her it saves you time and effort, and let her know she did a great job. If you receive compliments on a new outfit, call the store manager where you bought the clothes and pass the compliment along. Businesses usually do not hear from their customers unless there is a problem, so the manager will really love hearing what you have to say.

It's a simple thing, really, to pass along good thoughts, but it is something we rarely do. Doesn't it make you feel great when you receive a compliment for no reason—or when a stranger mentions you have a great smile or gorgeous eyes? I was wearing a new dress the other day and received two compliments from people I had never met—one at the gas station and the other in the library. I rarely wear dresses, but the way these strangers "put me up" with their compliments made me reconsider my wardrobe options.

A few years ago I was on a plane. As we were walking from the plane to the terminal, a man who apparently had been sitting a few rows behind me handed me a note. Here's what the note said:

I THINK YOU HAVE THE MOST BEAUTIFUL HAIR I HAVE EVER SEEN. WHATEVER YOU ARE DOING TO IT, KEEP IT UP, IT LOOKS WONDERFUL!

The man just handed me the piece of paper and kept on going. About a hundred feet ahead of me, he turned back to see my reaction, and just smiled and waved as he walked away, while I stood there dumbstruck. I don't know the man's name and have never seen him again, but I will remember him forever. He made a very ordinary person feel very special.

Since then I have handed out a few notes of my own to strangers. The compliment is always genuine; the sentiment is always real. Once you start looking for ways to "put people up" you will find many positive qualities in those around you that you may never have noticed before. The woman in the cubicle next to you may have a very melodious voice, the man selling newspapers on the street might wear stylish hats, or a neighbor could be an exceptionally compassionate person. Once you notice these things, instead of keeping your thoughts to yourself, share them with the other person. You might just make her feel so good that she goes out of her way to say something great to someone else.

Step 1: Put Six People Up

Every day this week "put six people up." Find something wonderful to say to them, but be sure the compliment is genuine. Some people will make you work to find something nice to say, but the idea is to find something great about everyone. After a while, you won't have to work so hard to make nice comments, you will automatically be looking for "put-ups," and verbalizing them will become second nature.

If there are other people in your household, be sure they are included in the put- ups. Often we forget to compliment those who are closest to us. We see what they don't do (i.e. the garbage wasn't taken out or homework wasn't completed) versus what they actually do. Compliments within the four walls of a home can dramatically improve the life within that home. Also, when we give praise, the person tends to develop the areas that were praised more than if we nagged them.

Step 2: Encourage Others

Tell those around you what you are doing and encourage them to adopt the "six a day" rule. Your goal by the end of the week is to get at least two other people putting-up six every day.

Step 3: Movie Time

The other part of this week's success plan is to watch the movie or read the book, *Pay it Forward*. Kevin Spacey, Helen Hunt, and Haley Joel Osment star in this great tale about a child whose final wish was for people not to pay back favors, but to pay them forward. It is a wonderful movie and is appropriate for the entire family. Watch alone, or with your partner, or get a group of people together and make it a celebration.

Week 14 Success Plan

* ✱ "Put six people up" every day
* ✱ Encourage others to put six people up
* ✱ Watch or read *Pay it Forward*

Week 15

FORGIVE AND MOVE ON

"The weak can never forgive. Forgiveness is the attribute of the strong." —Mahatma Gandhi

No one goes through life without someone hurting them—either intentionally or by accident. Some of those hurts are huge—parents abandoning children, acts of terrible violence, intentional cruelty. It is obvious and unfortunate that not all people are nice. But before you can really move on to bigger and better things in life, sometimes you have to forgive.

I think everyone knows a person who is so consumed with anger toward another person, or group of people, that it completely takes over their life. These people are missing out on so much because all their energy is focused on the anger and hatred they feel toward others. The reality is that bad stuff happens in life. Children die, women are raped, young men are shot and stabbed, loved ones commit suicide, and parents get cancer. In many ways this is not a very nice world. But you cannot let it overwhelm you, or you will miss all the good life has to offer.

Over the years I have known several people who obsess over little slights: a forgotten thank you, not being invited to an event, a caustic remark. It's all some people can talk about for years afterward. Just think how much more productive and happy he or she would be, if instead of being so preoccupied with small slights, they focused on helping the homeless, or tutored a child, or read to the blind . . . or just forgave the person and moved on.

My son's father left us when my son was an infant. I had fifteen dollars, a five-week old baby, no phone and no job. I was living in a mobile home out in the country, miles from the nearest store. A few years later he sued me for custody, claiming I was an unfit parent when he hadn't seen his son, or paid child support, in years. I am still paying the legal bills from that, even though Colby is now grown. Was I angry? Absolutely. Other words and emotions that come to mind are furious, unfair, heartbroken, panic, shock, and distress. There were a lot more, but they have faded over time.

The reality of the situation threw me into survival mode. I had a baby; we had to eat. I found a freelance job I could work from home until Colby was old enough to go into day care. When Colby was a few months old I was fortunate to find a local grandmother who cared for children in her home. I went back to work, and for almost three years I worked three jobs: a full time day job, a freelance writing job with the local newspaper and a weekend job doing graphic design that I could do at home. The early years of my son's evenings were spent at town council meetings and local events I was covering for the paper. But we were together, we were eating, and that was all that mattered.

At that time, I had not yet been able to forgive his father, but while I was working toward that, I got on with my life. Looking back, I learned a great deal. I learned how strong I was. I learned that simple moments with those you love are the important moments in life. I learned to do without and then appreciated all the more that which I did have. The lessons from this experience were countless and have all contributed to making me who I am today. It was a very tough time, but in some ways I am grateful for the experience, for it showed me how much I am truly capable of being.

While I was never consumed with my anger, it took me many years to be able to forgive. Over time, I was finally able to realize that Colby's dad had not developed many parenting or relationship skills. We learn by example and his childhood did not offer him scores of opportunities to learn. He did not know how to cope. Understanding that, I was finally able to forgive him. My forgiveness does not mean I want to live that experience all over again; it does not mean I want this man back in my life. It does means that I truly wish him well. He's had many disadvantages to overcome and I hope life finally brings him peace and happiness.

This week you will find someone, or several someones, to forgive. There is no set rule about what kinds of actions need forgiveness. What and whom you need to forgive is up to you. Infidelity, lies, and betrayal are certainly actions that most people would be hurt by. Forgiveness for these kinds of acts could require significant time and effort. On the other hand, little things such as forgetting a birthday, chronic lateness, or failing to follow through on a project may, in certain circumstances, also hurt a person profoundly. Only you know the specifics of how you have been hurt, and who hurt you in what way. If you look into your heart, you know what and whom you need to forgive.

Understand that forgiveness does not mean putting yourself back in the same situation that hurt you in the first place. In some more extreme cases, particularly those involving abuse or people who are unstable, it might not be safe to let the person who hurt you know they have been forgiven. But you can forgive them all the same. Some actions will take years to work through and forgive; others will be much easier to let go.

Step 1: Determine Whom and What to Forgive

Take some time this week to think about people who have hurt you in the past. Then choose several to forgive. Maybe you've been harboring a grudge against an uncle for a number of years over an argument that happened at a holiday gathering. While you've been cordial to him since then, you've also kept your distance. Or you could have been overlooked for a promotion and are secretly furious with your boss. There are any number of "wrongs" throughout our life that can benefit from forgiveness. Remember that other people are human, too. Others have their own good points and failings just as we do. People are not perfect. Focus this week on a few people you feel you need to forgive.

Step 2: Learn from the Situation

Many times, time and distance lend perspectives that have not before been considered. Find a few minutes each day this week to think about the circumstances surrounding who and whatever hurt you. Think about what the other person was dealing with in her life. Bear in mind her background and history. Try to understand her point of view. After considering all of this, you might still feel she is an insensitive jerk. And that's okay, because no matter how many bad feelings you have toward her, you will not change her. She will still be an insensitive jerk. Let it go. You have better, more productive things, to do with your life.

Forgiving someone is much easier said than done. It is hard to forgive. Very hard. But you have to do it if you are to fully enjoy your life. As with my son's father, there are other people who have not done right by me. But it is neither healthy nor productive to play the victim. Instead, I think about each time I was hurt and decide what I learned from it.

Every situation has some knowledge you can gain. The knowledge might be that you can't trust a certain person, or that a person doesn't make good decisions, or that a person isn't reliable. You could learn that a particular person can be violent, or that he doesn't always tell the truth. You might even learn something about yourself. Sometimes the knowledge is even enough to keep you from making the same mistake twice, and that's good.

Step 3: Forgive and Move On

You have to make a conscious decision to forgive, and once you've done that—truly forgiven somebody—you are free to move on. Depending on the situation and circumstances, you might want to tell the person you've forgiven him. And you might not. Keep in mind and appreciate the education you received from the situation.

If you are forgiving a person who is in regular contact with you, such as a family member or co-worker, you may have to set boundaries on the relationship. I once had a client who would get drunk and call me in the middle of the night. I was very angry with him for interrupting my sleep, and angry with myself for talking with him the first time or two. I had to have a strong working relationship with him during the day, so I made it quite clear that I liked him as a person, I wanted to work with him professionally and if he needed to call me in the middle of the night because his bus broke down, that was acceptable. To call me when he was drunk and morose was not. I did what I could to get him some help for his alcohol problems. And I forgave him because I knew he was dealing with some tragic personal issues, but it was not productive for me to either allow the behavior to continue, or to dwell on it.

Everyone forgives differently. You may want to have a symbolic ceremony where you write the names of people and their slights down on paper and then throw the paper (and the hurt they caused you) away. You might visualize the forgiveness enveloping the other person, or think about bundling your hurt in a laundry bag and washing the hurt away. I have a friend who pretends to toss her hurt out the car window. Or you may wish to simply learn from your experience and move on.

Once you have forgiven, you will be able to focus more freely on all the fun and positive activities life has to offer.

Week 15 Success Plan

* Find people in your life that you need to forgive
* Examine the situation and learn from it
* Decide how to handle that person in the future
* Forgive and move on

Week 16
R•E•S•P•E•C•T

"In my day, we didn't have self-esteem, we had self-respect, and no more of it than we had earned." —Jane Haddam

There is a huge difference between respecting someone and idolizing them. You may love Jennifer Lopez movies and think she is really cool, but do you respect her? Is she really a role model? Most of us are not qualified to say, as we only know the public Jennifer and not the real person. We do not know what she is dealing with on a day-to-day basis and decisions that might look like poor choices to us, may in fact be valid if we saw the big picture of her life.

When I was a young teen I idolized a beautiful young woman who was very successful. She had the best clothes, won a lot of awards and eventually got a wonderful job. Her life was perfect, or so I thought. I wanted to be just like her. One day I saw my idol at a local event and I breathlessly inched next to her as she was standing with a few other women. I was hoping that some of her perfection would rub off on me as I listened to her talk. But I listened instead with a growing horror, because the more my perfect idol spoke, the more I realized she was as dumb as a bag of hammers. This woman did not have a thought of her own. When she listened to other people, I watched as she hung on every word that every person said. I got the feeling that if others weren't walking her through every single step of her life that her life would come to a screeching halt, as she could not think what to do next. She was like a robot with a remote control.

At one time I idolized this woman because I thought she was a great role model, but after getting to see her in action, I changed my mind because I realized she was a puppet, and had not earned my respect. I had learned the difference. Just because you think a girl is cool does not mean she deserves your respect.

So what does it take for someone to earn your respect? To earn mine he would have to live his life with integrity, and do the right thing when the right thing needed to be done. He would have to put others before himself, and be a role model for those who were coming up behind him. He would have to be responsible, reliable, and compassionate. In short, he'd have to wear some very big shoes. That's my criteria; yours will probably be different.

As I have gone through my life, I found that while I could find very few people to respect completely (my mother being one), there were individual areas in many people I could admire. I completely respected a friend's commitment to her children, and the patience a local Boy Scout leader had with his pack. I respected my neighbor's commitment to caring for her ailing mother, one colleague's financial struggles, and another's compassion for a homeless man. I found I could have a high opinion in one area of a person's life, and disagree with another area, but still find some measure of respect.

I soon found something I could respect in virtually everyone I met and that was an important discovery. With rare exception, every person—and every living being—deserves some level of respect. You may not always agree with all of their thoughts or actions, but if you look, there is something about them that you can find to admire. This is important because respect affects how you deal with people and how you treat others. You are more likely to do right by those you respect than those you do not.

This week you will find qualities to respect about many different people you know. And, you will find respect for yourself. In your quest to become the best you that you can be, you deal with a unique set of circumstances every day. Each day is an exciting new adventure because it brings fresh challenges to earn the respect of others—and yourself.

Step 1:
Develop Your Marvel Meter and Your Dis Directory
Before you can respect anyone, you will have to do some soul searching to understand what criteria a person should display to earn your respect, and to what level. You might be proud to work for your boss because she is a great leader--motivating you and your department in fun and innovative ways. But you also know she cheats on her husband so you can't respect her completely.

First, make a list of the principles you admire in others. This will be your Marvel Meter and is a record of all the personal character traits you think are marvelous, and thus worthy of respect. Qualities on this list might be timeliness, loyalty, faithfulness, dependability, and integrity.

Now make another list of the attributes you don't respect. This is your Dis Directory. Being dishonest, disrespectful, disagreeable, discourteous, and disdainful might land on this list. Of course, not every word on this list has to begin with the letter D.

There are no right or wrong attributes to add to either list. These lists are entirely yours and reflect the traits that you most admire—and those you don't. But you may wish to consult with a few other people to find more attributes to add to each list. Be sure to decorate the lists and make them fun to look at. After your lists are complete, mentally review the people who are closest to you and assign them spots on the Marvel Meter and the Dis Directory. If you are like most people only a few of whom you list will land completely on the Marvel Meter, a few more completely on the Dis Directory, with most of the people you know falling somewhere in between.

Step 2: Learn From Those You Respect

The Marvel Meter and Dis Directory are educational tools to help you determine the attributes you admire in others and identify the people you truly respect. Think about the people who landed fully on the Marvel Meter. Why, for example, do you respect your dad so much? What is it specifically that makes you respect your closest friend? How, precisely, does he conduct himself during hard times, when tough decisions have to be made, or under stress? Why do you find the actions of your boss admirable? If someone on your Marvel Meter is close to you, ask her to lunch or over for coffee for the sole purpose of telling her that you respect her and give her the reasons why. A letter or email is also an option. You will totally make her day and give her added incentive to raise the bar for herself.

Also think about one person who landed solidly on the Dis Directory. Are you in a position to help her overcome some of her failings? Or does seeing specifically how you feel about her laid out in black and white make you want to reevaluate your relationship and set new boundaries? Know that you can learn from both the good and the not-so-good in people.

Step 3: Respect Yourself

Now that you have a handle on what respect means to you, it's time to find your own self-respect. Go back to your Marvel Meter and your Dis Directory. Look at the character attributes you listed and realistically look at each one in relation to you. In what areas do you conduct your life with honor and integrity? What areas could use a little more effort? What individual attributes do you respect in others that are especially difficult for you? Understand that no one is perfect and that this is merely a tool to help you raise the bar for you and your life.

Do something special for yourself in celebration of all the positive attributes of yours that landed on the Marvel Meter. Buy yourself a new jacket, go to a movie, or do something you have wanted to do for a long time, but could never find a reason to take the time. The Marvel Meter is proof that you are an awesome individual and are getting more incredible each and every day!

Step 4: Commit to Change

You probably have at least one attribute that landed on the Dis Directory. Make a commitment today to actively work toward changing that element of your life. Think about why you act or respond in a way that you find less than attractive. Recognize the signs and stresses that bring on the behavior or action and actively commit to a better response. If you realize that you tend to be spiteful toward your brother, take time to understand why you respond to his words or actions that way. Then find a better response such as humor or compassion. Visualize a scenario with your brother and picture yourself responding to your spiteful feelings with a new, more appropriate way. The next time you are actually with your brother, you will have a solid plan to deal with these negative feelings.

As time goes on and you are able to take more and more of your own attributes off your Dis Directory and put them on your Marvel Meter you will find that your life is richer and more fulfilling. Your respect level for yourself will grow because you are acting with more honor and integrity every single day. Your self-confidence will grow, and instead of you telling others how and why you respect them, others will be telling you.

Week 16 Success Plan

* Develop a Marvel Meter and a Dis Directory
* Match attributes of people you know with items on the Marvel Meter and Dis Directory
* Learn from those you respect—and those you don't
* Let those you admire know how you feel, and why
* Match your own attributes with the items on your lists
* Celebrate all the positive things you are
* Commit to changing at least one negative behavior

Week 17

FINDING COMMON GROUND

"Why cannot we work at cooperative schemes and search for the common ground binding all mankind together?"
—William Orville Douglas

As difficult as it is to find things in common with people who are different from you, it is sometimes even harder to find common ground with those closest to you. People are often more emotional around those they know well, and when tempers rise and tears start to flow, common ground can turn into a mud slide.

How well do you know the people around you—people who are your family, people you work with regularly, your friends? Do you know your in-laws well, or is it more of a superficial relationship? Do you know the dreams, desires and goals of your sister? How about your grandparent's thoughts on political issues, the environment, technology and pop culture? What is your son's favorite color, your mother's fondest memory, or your best friend's dream vacation spot? Do you know whom your teenage daughter considers her best friend, or who in your social circle your husband absolutely can't stand?

These questions are important because the answers give you insight to who that person is. In today's world we all get so caught up in our own lives that we forget to nurture our relationships with the most important people in our lives, the people who are around us every day. Today's divorce rate is one of the highest in history. Parents often don't know who their children really are. You work with the same people every day for years on end, but do you know what they are thinking?

One of the reasons many people do not get along is they cannot find ways to relate with one another. They cannot find any common ground. Husbands and wives fall out of love because common ground slips away, and parents grow apart from their children because they don't dig deep enough to find common interests.

It goes without saying that people who have established strong common bonds work better together, stay together longer as families, and maintain friendships that last a lifetime. Those who fail to reach out—who miss the opportunity to find those similar threads—miss that all-important one-on-one connection.

A few years ago I dated a man my son absolutely could not stand. He tried to find common ground with Colby by talking about or offering activities that interested him when he was a teen. But he never once sat down with Colby and asked about his interests. He assumed that what interested him as a teen would interest Colby. He was making a sincere effort, but was going about it the wrong way.

The problem is that in our online society, we have lost a lot of our communication skills. We are losing the ability to talk with one another and often don't have a clue how to begin conversation with people we barely know.

The first occasion on which I spent any length of time with Johnny PayCheck was when I picked him up after a show in west central Tennessee. His bus had broken down in South Dakota and he had flown in for an acoustic performance, leaving his band and road crew back with the bus. When we left the venue it was after midnight and it was pouring rain. On a good day, it was a two-hour drive back to Nashville; on this night it would take over four.

As I was driving out of the little town, I was trying to think of something to say to John. In music circles he was, after all, a living legend. Before taking John on as a client, I had read over his file in the library at the Country Music Hall of Fame and while it gave more information than even I wanted to know about his career, it didn't say much about who Johnny PayCheck was as a person. But, from what I could gather, we really didn't have much in common. I had grown up in the 1960s, an only child in a fairly stable middle class environment in suburban Minnesota and had done well in school. John had spent his childhood in Ohio in the forties, had to scramble for whatever he could get, dropped out in the seventh grade, and was playing in bars and clubs not too long after that. What on Earth, I wondered, could we possibly have in common?

Just as the rainy silence was getting more than a little uncomfortable an impressive strike of lightening lit up an old farmhouse.

"Look at that," I said, moved by the surreal sight.

"Boy, I bet that farm house has a lot of stories to tell," answered John.

The dam had burst. From there, one subject led to another as we talked about architecture and farming, family histories and antiques, dogs and horses, children and education, music and books. We discussed philosophy and spirituality, and politics and travel, and the one thought I had as I drove through the rain, was that Johnny PayCheck and I were not all that different. We both loved dogs and our children. We liked the peace and quiet of the country at times, and the lights of the city at others. We found differences of opinion, of course, but we had established enough common ground that we were able to respect the differences as much as we embraced the common threads of our lives.

Throughout my association with John, that one evening set the stage for numerous interesting discussions. Sometimes he'd call me from the road after a show, not to talk music, but to see what I thought about the news of the day, or some off the wall subject that had popped into his mind. Because of the common ground we had been able to find, John often did interviews or made personal appearances for me that I knew he really did not want to do. And because we had found areas in common, we could speak far more frankly with each other than I could with many of my other public relations clients, where our relationship was more formal. If John didn't immediately see the value in something I thought would be good for his career, we discussed it and more often than not, he ended up doing it. Common ground aided both my business and Johnny Paycheck's career.

This week you will initiate discussion to find common ground with people around you, especially those with whom you have drifted apart. Remember, if you dig deep enough, you can find something in common with just about anyone, including a teenaged son or a standoffish sister. The trick is where to dig and how deep to go.

Step 1: Choose Your Subjects

You are probably aware of several relationships in your life where you and another person have grown apart. Sometimes that is a natural progression of life. Children grow up and leave home, co-workers change jobs, neighbors move across the country. Other times such a transition leaves an awkward void at the dinner table or in staff meetings. So choose one or two people that you really would like to bring back more fully into your life.

Before you talk with the person, spend some time thinking about the circumstances that drew you apart. Why are you not as close as you once were? What are the problems, if any, in the relationship and what do you see bringing the two of you closer together?

Step 2: Start Talking

It takes two to have a conversation, but it only takes one to begin. First choose your moment—you can't really plan these things, but you'll know when it is right. Often the other person will give you a lead-in by making a comment about a program on television, or something you pass while in the car. Good comebacks to their comments are words such as: "Yes, what do you think about that?" "How do you think that happened?" or "I agree with that, but I know you have a different perspective and I am interested to hear your thoughts."

Notice that you are not judging, you are just asking his thoughts. That is one way to get to know someone a little better—to find out what he thinks and at the same time not criticize his answers.

If he doesn't offer an opening comment, you might break the ice by saying something like, "I saw the most interesting segment on the news today." Then explain the news item and ask for his thoughts. Other openers are to ask people their preference about something, such as computer desks or wall colors or steaks, and why they prefer that choice to another. Even though it's sometimes hard to get them started, people generally like to talk about themselves and their opinions.

As the person talks, your only job is to listen. And in the listening, no matter how far apart the two of you seem, you will eventually hear some thoughts and ideas that echo your own. Suddenly, your little piece of common ground has grown that much more. Additionally, in areas in which you do not agree, you may have deeper understanding of where the person is coming from, and they you.

Step 3: Go Slowly

If you and the other person have grown apart, it may take some time to rebuild the relationship. You need to realize that the other person may not want to re-establish anything, but if he is family, or a co-worker, and you will be seeing him regularly, over time the tenuous bond will become less strained if you occasionally ask for an opinion or preference. Follow through by really considering the answers. Once the other person realizes he is not being judged by his responses, he will likely open up more and more, bringing you closer to the inside circle of his life. Eventually you may even re-establish enough common ground to have meaningful conversations, and some of these conversations could provide wonderful moments you will remember forever.

* Choose several people to bring back to the inner fold
* Encourage conversation by commenting on ideas or events and asking their opinions
* Listen, rather than judge
* Go slowly and let the relationship build
* Find common ground and enjoy your differences

JUDGMENT DAY

"None are more unjust in their judgments of others than those who have a high opinion of themselves."—Charles H. Spurgeon

Y ou are the only person on the planet who is walking in your shoes. Isn't that mind-boggling? Just imagine: absolutely no one else is dealing with the same background, the same people, and the same exact set of circumstances that you are. No one but you has any idea what your true triumphs and tragedies are, just as you have no idea of the triumphs and tragedies of anyone else. If you think along those lines it becomes very difficult to judge another person.

A year or so ago I edited a manuscript titled *Both Sides Now* that was an autobiography of a man named Dhillon Khosla. Dhillon was born overseas to a German mother and a father who was from India. He grew up on the east coast and graduated from law school at the top of his class. He currently is a very respected senior attorney for the 9th Circuit Court of Appeals. The one detail that makes Dhillon a little unusual is the fact that he spent the first twenty-eight years of his life as a woman. Dhillon has endured many operations to physically transition from female to a fully functioning male.

Now when most of us are confronted with the words "sex change" or "transgendered" our first assumption is to think the person is a bit strange. We automatically assume that the person is weird, that there is something a little off about them and, curiosity aside, we all feel a bit uncomfortable because what kind of person would go through such a long and painful transition? And why?

In editing Dhillon's manuscript I saw first hand how difficult life was for him when he was female. From the time he was a little girl he identified as a male. As a child he didn't understand why he was always grouped with the girls. And as he matured, Dhillon felt a kinship with men and a clear difference when he was around women. In his mind he was male, and as most men are, he was attracted to women. There have been recent medical studies that show there is a point in the early stage of development when the child is still in the uterus where the body and brain develop gender. In Dhillon's case, as in the case of the many other people who are transgendered, the brain developed as one gender and the body developed as another. Science and modern medicine have now combined to fix what many now consider to be nothing more than a birth defect.

In talking to Dhillon, and in watching him, there is nothing remotely female about him. He looks, walks, talks, and thinks like a man. He is intelligent and well spoken. Any judgment about Dhillon that I might have had evaporated after I read the first page of his manuscript. As inconceivable as it would be for me to transition to a male gender, I understand not only why Dhillon transitioned, but also that for him there was no other choice.

I have no way of knowing what my choice would be if I were wearing Dhillon's shoes, because Dhillon's circumstances are unique to Dhillon. You and I have other circumstances that we deal with every day and we make our choices of actions and behaviors based on those circumstances. Even though we might be friends who talk regularly about each other's lives, I can't experience what you are going through and you can't live my experiences through my eyes.

Thank goodness that most of us do not have to deal with decisions as major as the ones that Dhillon made. Our decisions are more likely to do with work, parenting, relationships or family issues. If I don't agree with a decision you make regarding your children, I can't judge you. I can tell you I either support or don't support you. I can tell you why I feel either way, but I can't judge you, because I am not living your life. I do not know all the circumstances surrounding your decision. I am not breathing your air, or living your personality, history, heritage, family life, economics, or dreams.

There are instances every day where we make decisions about other people: this person is shy, this one can't be trusted, this person doesn't handle money well, this one is loyal. But there is a difference in making a decision about a woman and judging her. This is important, so I will say it again. Making a decision about someone and judging a him are two separate concepts.

You probably know of someone who is a little different. Here in Nashville we have a man who stands on a certain street corner all day every day and waves at cars. On first glance, that is a little odd. You assume that the man is one brick shy of a load, and that certainly may be true. It is also possible that he is retired and has nothing better to do with his day than smile and wave at people. He could be independently wealthy and on a mission to make people happy, because everyone who sees him drives away with a bemused look on their face. There is a slim possibility that he could be undercover for the FBI. He could also be just what he seems, an odd person who waves at cars. There are many things this man could be, but to assume something and make a judgment on that assumption is unfair.

You may also have a friend who makes a decision you think is wrong. Years ago many people thought I was crazy to quit my steady, stable job to open my own business. After all, I had a young child to support. But being available for school events and field trips and being able to take my son to the doctor without worrying that I would lose my job were far more important to me than money. I gave up steady and stable in exchange for time with my son, all the time realizing that there were many good arguments for steady and stable. For me and for my circumstances, I made the right decision. It may not have been the right decision for anyone else, but I know without a doubt it was right for us.

This week you will attempt to wear the shoes of another person and try to view life through their eyes.

Step 1: Live Through Someone Else's Eyes

Remember when you were a child and played cowboys and Indians, or princess bride? At one time or another we've all pretended we were someone else. Now you will finally have the chance! Choose several people you have seen recently in the news. It doesn't matter what your news source is: television, radio, newspaper, magazine, newsletter or the Internet. You can choose a teacher who was fired over a discipline problem, an elected official who made an unpopular zoning decision, a celebrity whose behavior was particularly outrageous, or any one else who interests you.

Step 2: Feel Their Pain

We've all at some time been judged unfairly and know how much that can hurt. It is now your job to view the news item from another perspective, not the spin that the media put on it, but the possible thoughts of the person you chose, and their reasoning leading up to the incident. Visualize the circumstances surrounding the event. Where did it happen? What is the history behind the event? Who were the key players and what were their roles? What had happened to the key people just prior to the incident? There is no way for you to know all the details, so guess as best you can.

For example, a boy who was arrested for shoplifting could have a mental disorder. He might be broke and desperately need the stolen item. Perhaps he was dared by a friend, or maybe it was an undercover test of store security. The idea is to open your mind to possibilities other than the obvious, for things are not always as they seem. Have fun with your ideas and try to come up with ten different scenarios for each incident or event. You might even brainstorm with friends to see who can come up with the most plausible story or the most outrageous one.

It could be that you will never agree with what the person in your news item did to land in the news, but you may come to understand that there are other sides to every story and that the people involved could have had valid reasoning for whatever they did.

Step 3: Localize

Repeat steps one and two closer to home and apply it to your own life. Maybe your six-year-old son was sent to the principal's office because he hit another child. Take some extra time to understand the situation from your son's point of view. Visualize what his day is like at school. View his classroom from his desk. Who are the children who sit around him? There obviously was a compelling reason for his visit to the principal, but maybe he was provoked. It is possible he was defending himself. Maybe he was tired or frustrated about something. It doesn't make his actions right, but knowing the story from his side may make a difference in what you do about it. He has to learn that his behavior was not acceptable, but how you get that lesson across should depend as much on why he acted as he did, as the action itself.

Week 18 Success Plan

* Live through another's eyes by analyzing decisions or events in the news
* Visualize the circumstances surrounding the event
* Have fun determining all possibilities for whatever happened
* Localize the idea and try to find possible reasons for events in your own life

CONSTRUCTIVE CRITICISM

"Criticize not to punish, but to correct something that is hampering success." —Coach John Wooden

Michael Mahler is the bandleader of a group called Wild Horses, who are former clients of mine. In the early stages of their career, before they were on Epic records, we did a lot of media training. This included what to say to the press and how to say it, what to wear during the interview, how to sit while on-camera, and how not to talk all at the same time. Actually, much of my public relations career was built around coaching people to eat, drink, sit, look, walk, and talk like a celebrity. Then when the real deal came along—a real interview with a real reporter—my clients were ready.

After each interview was over, we'd critique it. Did each member accomplish his or her goals? Were the answers clear and concise? Did one person speak at a time? Was the reporter confused about anything? If so, why?

I operated on the assumption that no matter how well anyone did, there was always room for improvement. And there was. There was always something someone could have done better, but I was careful not to minimize any accomplishments in the interview or shake any newfound confidence.

All four members of Wild Horses were—and are—naturals at talking to the press. My job was simply to take what was good and make it better, but to do that we had to discuss what the band was doing in their interviews that prevented all their goals from being reached. I must have done well, because Michael once said he had never met anyone who could tear him apart so badly and still make him feel so good. It's called constructive criticism and the key is that—in the words of John Wooden—criticism is not about punishment, instead criticism should be to correct something that is keeping you from your goals.

My agent, Sharlene Martin, thoroughly understands this concept. It is a defined skill to make people feel great about being helpfully critiqued and Sharlene knows exactly how to do it. She is very nurturing and uses inclusive phrases such as, "Maybe we can," and "Let's think about," rather than the more personal and negative "You need to" or "Must you always . . ." Her inclusive phrases keep authors from feeling isolated and alone, and in her guidance and counseling of authors she makes them feel motivated and wonderful about themselves. Sharlene understands that people respond better to praise than to criticism. But, if you praise while critiquing, both goals are accomplished: the author feels great and Sharlene is able to steer their written work toward a better end result.

Words are the key. It is not so much as what you say, as how you say it. The study of the effects of positive and negative words on people is fascinating. In one recent study, researchers from North Carolina State University in Raleigh studied memory retention when people were presented positive and negative words about aging. Older people remembered less when presented with negative associations than they did with positive ones, and people of all ages performed equally well when presented with just positive associations.

Many other scientific studies have shown that people respond better to positive words than negative ones. I know from personal experience that if a friend says to me, "Don't forget your hat," I do not remember the negative admonition of "don't" and I will "forget my hat." If, on the other hand, the same friend says, "Remember your hat," I do.

We all use negative words every day. Nor do we realize how much these words affect our performance in all that we do. Telling a child that she can't go out and play because she did a terrible job picking up her room is not productive. Remember to critique positively and instead say something like: "I saw you picked up two books off the floor. That's great, I am so proud of you! Now before you go out to play, you can pick up the rest of the toys in your room."

Which would you respond better to: a blanket statement that you can't go out because you didn't finish doing something, or powerful praise followed by the fact that if you now do something, you can go out to play?

This week you will consciously work toward speaking in positive ways. Words such as no, don't, can't, and won't, will be weeded from your vocabulary. And, you will choose one person to totally pump up with your positive words.

Step 1: Weed the Words

This week attempt to weed all the negative words from your vocabulary. It will be harder than you think because we use these words all the time so you may need some moral support from those around you. It might also help to post a note on your refrigerator, your computer or your mirror to help you remember to use positive words. Here are some ideas to help you rephrase your words:

Instead of "don't forget to" say "remember to"
Instead of "you need to" say "let's talk about"
Instead of "don't do that" say "try this"
Instead of "I won't" say "instead, I could"
Instead of "why don't you" say, "I think you" or "maybe you"

"Don't" will be the hardest to weed out as we all use it dozens of times every day. Have fun finding creative ways of speaking around the word and make it a personal challenge to go an entire day without saying, "don't."

If you find yourself saying "no" a lot, especially when children are into something they shouldn't, say "oops" instead and offer an alternative to what they are doing.

Step 2: Speak Positively
Once you have weeded the negative words out of your life, it will be easy to speak in positive phrases all the time. Saying "would you please," "we can," and "I'd rather" replace their negative counterparts and give those around you a more optimistic outlook. Make a point to leave anyone you come in contact with—either in person, or over the phone or Internet—thinking positively about you and your interaction with them. Make them feel good about talking with you by using positive phrases. This can be an especially fun challenge for families or co-workers—having everyone attempt to eliminate negative words.

Step 3: Pump Someone Up

Here comes the exciting part. This week you will also choose to help someone who needs to improve his or her self-esteem. This person could be a child in your classroom, a co-worker, a family member, or even a clerk at a retail location you frequent—anyone who you think needs a little positive motivation to gain confidence.

Maybe your daughter's self-esteem needs a little building up. Without telling her what you are doing, say something positive as often as possible. "You did a great job on that paper," "I really liked the way you handled that situation," "I'm interested in hearing your ideas for . . .," "Thank you for helping," "I appreciate you always being on time," "I think you are just the person to do this." Many times, under normal circumstances, you would have said nothing to her at all, so she may be a little startled to hear herself complimented in such a positive way.

At the end of the week, see if you notice a difference in whomever you chose—the way she walks or talks, her attitude, or the way she presents herself. More than likely you will notice an amazing difference. Know that the difference is you—you just changed someone's life for the better! Keep feeding positive words and this difference will last forever.

It is an incredible concept to understand that you can positively motivate a person to do a better job or to get more out of life. You did a great job and should be jumping up and down, so be sure to do something special to celebrate.

Week 19 Success Plan

* Weed negative words from your vocabulary
* Learn to speak positively to everyone
* Choose someone to pump up
* Notice the difference and celebrate

LIFE IS NOT FAIR

"Life is never fair, and perhaps it is a good thing for most of us that it is not." —Oscar Wilde

Working in the entertainment industry for twenty years has shown me how grossly unfair life can be. Very talented singers often sit back and watch as others, who may be less talented, land a record deal just because they have more financial backing. Other artists who already have a record deal might be pushed to the background or even lose their deal because an artist with more star power hits the charts the same time as they do, or the record label consolidates and lays off their producer. The reasons for failure are endless and have absolutely nothing to do with the talent of an individual artist. None of the reasons have anything to do with fair.

It's the same in virtually every life situation or industry. I have an extremely intelligent friend who bounced from one low-paying job to another for years, watching as his friends one by one embarked on great careers. Then, just as he finally got a great job, the company folded. Fortunately, another company picked him up and he has since been promoted several times, but it was very frustrating for him to have been passed over for lesser qualified talent so many times.

Brenda Bagull owns a successful print shop, but it was only after years of working one menial job after the other that she was able to move from employee to owner. Brenda is extremely bright, but as a child, she did not have the advantages of money and education. Despite her intellect, it was disheartening for her to watch others achieve their goals, while she struggled so much harder than others did.

Superstar or ordinary Joe, it really is heartbreaking to watch as a younger, or less talented, person gets promoted while you do not. It's annoying when you lose out on something due to circumstances you could not control. It hurts when someone you care for treats others better than they do you. Life sometimes is just not fair and we all need to learn to deal with that fact. If you can accept that unfairness is part of life, then you can move on to the next step, which is making the best of it.

I recently met an older gentleman in the office of our local electric company. I was opening an office for a client and needed to pay the deposit. The woman at the information desk directed me to a waiting area where five or six other people were sitting. And when I say sitting, that's exactly what they were doing. These people were sitting, staring straight ahead with blank expressions on their faces, the ladies with their purses on their laps. Granted, the electric company is not my favorite choice of places to spend an afternoon either, but I found it interesting that everyone was so alike in their postures of bored resignation. As I was noticing this, an older man came in to pay his deposit. He stood in front of our little group, spread his arms wide and proclaimed in a loud voice, "It's a wonderful day! What is everyone so glum about?" He went around smiling and shaking hands, which the people did very politely before resuming staring straight ahead.

The man ended up sitting near me and sharing a story. His roommate had become ill a few months before and quickly became permanently disabled. Because the room-mate couldn't work, his car was repossessed. The man and the roommate rode to work together and because the roommate was ill and the car had been taken, this man lost his job. Because he lost his job and had no transportation to look for work, he had no money and they both soon lost their apartment. The roommate went to live with a distant relative in another city, but this man had no family and became homeless.

He quickly realized that life on the streets was not for him and found his way to a social services agency that helped homeless people find employment. The agency found a group home for him to live in and a night job doing janitorial work that was near enough to walk to. After several months he had saved up enough money to rent a furnished efficiency apartment and he was there to pay his electrical deposit.

After all the unfairness that life dealt this man, he still woke up with a big smile on his face, took time to listen to other people's troubles and help them when he could. He still felt that every day, no matter what, was a good day. What impressed me most was that even though he didn't quite understand why life had been so unfair, he didn't take a moment to wallow in his misery. He just kept trudging along, looking for opportunities.

As he told me, if he hadn't kept trying to help himself, he'd still be homeless—just as Brenda Bagull would not own a print shop if she hadn't just kept plugging away.

Knowing how life can sometimes knock you flat on your back, it is important to be as fair as you can in dealing with other people. Everyone needs to stand up for themselves and get the best deal possible, but if this wonderful deal is at the expense of another, then the deal isn't really so wonderful. Truly great negotiators try to envision the other parties wants and needs, and creatively offer extras that they think will sweeten the pot without compromising their own deal.

Here's an example. I once was negotiating with the IRS on reducing a client's back taxes. He owed several tens of thousands of dollars and had about ten percent of that to pay on this bill. Through discussion with the IRS rep I learned that their big concern was not so much the back taxes, but that my client, who was fairly young, completely understand that he must stay current on all his taxes in the future. With that in mind, I was able to negotiate a full settlement for one-tenth of the back bill, with the condition that my client remain current on all quarterly payments for the next five years. If he didn't stay current and defaulted, then the other nine-tenths of his back taxes were due immediately. My client got what he wanted, complete settlement with the limited amount of funds he had to work with, and the IRS got what they wanted, a tax-paying citizen who was guaranteed to pay on time. Everyone was happy.

This week you will learn to stop and look at both sides of the issue before you make a decision. You will stop and think, really think, about the fairest solution.

Step 1: Take a Trip Down Memory Lane

Think of several times when life or people treated you unfairly. View the memory from your standpoint, then switch roles and think of the situation from the other side. If your car broke down and you missed a big job interview, is it possible that you did not maintain the car properly?

If you were in an accident and the other person was completely at fault, is there anything you could have done to avoid the incident? If a friend abandoned you in time of need, try to understand what was going on in their life at the same time. Look at these situations as an opportunity to learn, not as a smack-yourself-upside-the-head kind of punishment.

Step 2: Look at the Long Term Consequences

Now look at the long-term consequences of whatever you found to be unfair. It is possible that with a little time and perspective the situation no longer looks quite as unfair. It is possible that big job interview you missed wasn't such a big deal after all. The company could have folded later on or been bought out with your position being eliminated. The car accident may have prevented something worse from happening. The person who dumped you so cruelly might have gone on to show some very unstable sides of his or her personality, so it was ultimately good that you didn't stay together.

Step 3: Bring out the Costumes

Next, look at an event or situation that is currently happening in your life or has happened recently. Maybe your teenage daughter thinks it's unfair that you do not let her go to a party. Get together with her and switch roles. You pretend to be your daughter, and she pretends to be you. You each have one minute to give the other person background on your thoughts before you switch. Prior to switching roles you might say, "I am thirty-eight, happily married, and am concerned for the safety of my daughter because I love her very much and she is important to me. I am concerned about letting my daughter go to this party because I don't know who will be supervising, what activities they will be doing, what kinds of food and beverages will be served. I trust my daughter but I do not always trust her friends."

You could simply sit down and have a conversation, or make it fun and switch clothes or act out the actions and mannerisms of the other person. Some people even turn the idea into a spontaneous one-act play, complete with props. It is important to really get into the role of the other person and try to think of all their concerns from their perspective. Even if you do not have a role-playing partner, you can play both roles yourself.

If you think your boss passed you over for a promotion unfairly, recruit someone to play your boss, or even better, you play your boss and recruit a friend to play you. Sit at a desk just as your boss sits, talk and move like your boss. Take a moment to think about areas that must be his biggest concern: are there enough company funds to meet payroll this week, what repairs need to be made to the building, is there one employee who is stirring up dissention among the ranks, is his boss giving pressure for this division to perform better?

Once you get into the role switch, you will be able to better see yourself as others see you. Be prepared, as it may be an eye opener—for better or for worse! Use any information you learn about yourself—or the other person—as a tool to better understand both them and you. Once you have perspective from the other side, situations often do not seem as unfair.

Week 20 Success Plan

* Recall unfair events from your past and view them from all sides
* Look at unfair events from the perspective of time
* Role play with a partner or friend to better understand a current unfairness
* Make it fun with costumes and props
* Use what you learn about yourself and the other person to better yourself and your relationship

GIVING CREDIT WHERE CREDIT IS DUE

"Better to have one person working with you than three for you."
—Dwight D. Eisenhower

Singer and actor Randy Travis won the hearts of the entertainment community early in his career when he referred to his business decisions in the plural. In his interviews, he was always very complimentary of those around him, saying, "we thought," or "we decided." It was never "I," or "me." Randy had learned that launching a career does not happen by itself. As it takes a village to raise a child, it takes a team to launch a superstar.

In any celebrity's career, in addition to the celeb, there are the manager, agent, publicist, lawyer, hairdresser, wardrobe person, driver, mechanic, choreographer, sales and marketing team, producer, and a slew of other people—all of whom have input in some way or another to the career of the celebrity. Every one of these people has an important job to do because if even one person doesn't do their work, it causes a problem for everyone else.

Randy Travis understood right away that teamwork is necessary. Whether in business or in personal relationships, the "my way or the highway" attitude does not encourage others to go to bat for you, and we've all seen time after time the unhappiness that can occur when just one person rules the roost. Supporters, whether they are your family or your co-workers, are not expendable commodities. To win full support, you need to ask their advice, get their opinions, and actually consider both. Everyone wants to—and should be—valued, and more importantly, people should be recognized for their efforts.

It doesn't matter where a good idea comes from. If it comes from you, that's great. But if it comes from a co-worker, that's wonderful too because your supporters are part of your team; they are a part of you.

I find it energizing to know that there is more than one way to do just about anything. Have you ever noticed how different people bathe their dogs? Even if you go to a grooming shop, you will find as many ways to bathe a dog, as there are dogs. Some start at the head, others on the neck, and others at the feet or the tail. Some dogs are washed by one person; others by three or four. Everyone uses a different kind of soap, and some bathers don't use any soap at all. Some people use brushes to wash their dogs; others use sponges or cloths, or their hands. There are also about a thousand products to use for rinsing dogs, from vinegar, to products for human hair, to specially formulated canine products. Some people walk their dogs dry in the sun; others shun the sun. Some people blow-dry their dogs with a hair dryer, others don't. The only element that is consistent in all of this is that in the end, *all* the dogs are shiny and clean.

People do things the way they do because it works for them. But, you should recognize that what works for one person may not work for another—or for a group. To say there is a right or wrong way to wash a dog is ludicrous. There are dog trainers who have a certain dog washing method they follow, whether out of convenience, or habit or superstition. But you would hope that if an employee came up with a better way, the trainer would listen, consider the suggestion, and give recognition for the idea.

It gives people a huge sense of accomplishment to know they came up with something that works, and it might streamline your own efforts as well.

The difficulty in giving credit to others arises when a person you don't care for or are mad at actually has a good idea, or even worse, when someone else takes credit for your idea.

In the latter case, whether it is a boss or a co-worker or a sibling, it might be interesting to have a very casual hallway or kitchen table discussion with whomever took credit for your work. The idea here is to achieve two goals: a private acknowledgement that your efforts contributed, and to get the other person thinking—at least privately—that without you they would not have had success with the idea. You might start by congratulating your boss and add that you hoped incorporating your specific contribution into her plan helped. Then let her take it from there. You will find out very quickly what kind of a person she really is. The other benefit is that you know you are being the bigger person here.

If you are having difficulty accepting that a neighbor you can't stand or had a disagreement with had a great idea, pretend he is your best friend and give him the nicest compliment you can. At the very least it will surprise him, and it may just be the thing that puts any disagreement to rest.

This week you will look for creative ways to give credit to others. It doesn't take too long for the credit and acknowledgements to turn around and head right back toward you. Being recognized for your own efforts is almost as much fun as recognizing others.

Step 1: Seek Opportunities to Give Credit

When was the last time you really acknowledged the small fact that your son took out the trash? Hopefully you have thanked him for doing it. But wouldn't it encourage him even more if at some point you said to the whole family, "Doesn't the house look especially nice today? A lot of the credit should go to Jeff. Just think what the house would look and smell like if he didn't take out the trash."

That public acknowledgement will not only make Jeff swell with pride, but motivate the rest of the family to do things so they, too, can be publicly recognized.

This week see how much credit you can pass out to people. Instead of thanking your car mechanic, tell him or her that without them you would be stranded. Tell the dry cleaner about the compliments you receive on your shirts. Give the people around you the credit they deserve and you will be surprised at how great it males *you* feel.

Step 2: Be Open to New Ideas

Also stay especially alert this week for new ideas. Maybe your mother has a new idea about a way to celebrate a holiday. Automatically resisting her idea just because you've always celebrated a certain way could be a mistake. Yes, traditions are nice, but once in a while it is nice to expand the tradition, or start a new one.

If an employee has an idea for a new office procedure, really listen. Maybe it is not developed enough to implement yet, or maybe the idea is just not that great, but by thinking about a new procedure at all, that employee has shown that he cares about his office environment and has proved he is a dedicated person to have around.

Step 3: Credit Everyone

Here's the hard part—recognizing the efforts of someone you do not like, or who has proven themselves untrustworthy. This can be tough. I always try to put my feelings about the person aside and recognize the achievement by asking myself what I would say if he were someone I liked. Often, even that can be difficult, so I think up the nicest phrases I can about the achievement. "This proposal will save so much time," is one such phrase. Other phrases include, "I can't wait to get started on your new idea," or "I really think with this plan in place, anything is possible." The person that you do not like might even surprise you and return the compliment. Even better, you may get to know another side of him and realize that your differences are not all that great.

This week can be very amusing as you think up your own complimentary phrases. You can even enlist the aid of a friend and see who can come up with the most outrageous, the funniest, or the most gracious comments.

Week 21 Success Plan

* Look for opportunities to give credit to others
* Be open to new ideas
* See who can come up with the most unique phrases to credit others

Your New Best Friend

"A friend is one of the nicest things you can have, and one of the best things you can be." —Douglas Pagels

How many friends do you have—real tried and true friends you can call at three in the morning no matter what? I am fortunate in that I have many friends, but what is more important to me than they being my friend, is that I am their friend. I have the pleasure of helping them through tough times and the joy of celebrating their many successes.

Having friends around is important for many reasons. Friends support us when we are down. Friends help when we need it the most, and friends laugh and cry and walk and eat and play with us. We also learn and grow from our friends.

I never really considered the extent of my friendship with Jolene Mercer until my son ran away from home. This was several years ago and was not the first time he had run away. I was especially concerned this time as he was having some serious health issues and I knew he needed medical attention. Fortunately, we learned early on that he was still in the area. When Jolene heard of the situation, she dropped everything, put her business on hold and spent more than a week supporting me full time and donating her time and efforts to help find my son. Here's just a sample of what she did. She organized a network of more than fifty volunteers to comb the streets and feed information to her and to the police. She then directed groups of people to hang out in places where he had been seen. She called Colby's friends regularly, and even dressed as a bag lady and "infiltrated" the local homeless community. As the parent of a runaway, just to know that my son was alive and in the area was incredible. I have never forgotten what she did and will always call her friend.

Cheryl Brickey is another true friend. When, in a freak accident, a glass lamp fell across my face severing a facial artery and resulting in numerous stitches, Cheryl came over and spent hours cleaning up what amounted to several units of blood that had sprayed all over the house as I blindly searched for the phone so I could call 911. I am proud to call Cheryl a friend.

One trait that is common to most people who are considered "successful," both in the traditional and the non-traditional sense, is that the person has a diverse network of friends. This diverse group is invaluable in leading a successful person along the many different areas of their life.

Ricky Lynn Gregg is one such person, as he has never met a stranger. No matter what the situation, he knows someone. People he knows range from those in his Native American community, to those in the music world, to people from church, actors, politicians, and sports figures. He knows people who bake and sew, people who hunt and fish, people who are bankers and others who sell cars. The people he knows are rich and poor, black and white, red and yellow, city dwellers and country folk—and he calls them all friend.

Ivan Misner, founder and CEO of Business Network International, and the author of the *New York Times* bestseller, *Masters of Networking*, says, "One of the important keys to being successful at building a powerful personal network is that of diversity. It is human nature to congregate with people who are very much like us. The problem with this is that when we surround ourselves with people who have similar contacts, it may be difficult to make connections with new people or the companies we desire to do business with. The truth is, when it comes to networking, not having a lot in common with someone means that that person could well become a connector for you to a whole world of people that you might otherwise not have been be able to meet."

Ricky Lynn Gregg and Ivan Misner both know the power of a diverse network of friends. This is a week where you will revel in old friendships and kindle new ones—for one thing you can never have is too many friends.

Step 1: Identify Your Friends

Take time this week to make a mental list of your closest friends. These are the people who are your strongest supporters, the ones who will let you cry on their shoulder and who will rush to help when needed. After considering all the people who are close to you, you may find you have two really good friends or you may have twenty. However many, be sure to let each of them know they are one of your special friends with a quick letter, email or phone call. Your friends will feel treasured and you will feel pretty good yourself!

Step 2: Do Something Nice for an Old Friend

Now that you've identified these wonderful old friends, it is time to do something extraordinary for one or two of them.

Hopefully you have not had to assist your friends—or they you—in any capacity close to what Jolene and Cheryl did for me, but isn't it time you did something extra special for them? Here are a few ideas. If your friend has young children, offer to take the kids for a night or even a weekend so your friend can enjoy some personal time alone, or with her spouse. Organize a house cleaning party and clean a friend's home from top to bottom. Surprise a friend with tickets to a special event, such as a ballgame or a concert. Hand craft a gift card that expresses your appreciation for the friendship and give it to a friend on a day that is not a holiday. Gather a group together for a "roast" in honor of a friend. Here, many people can tell your friend how much he means to those around them. Treat a friend to a spa day or to another special place he has always wanted to visit. The ideas are endless.

Step 3: Cultivate a New Best Friend

Every year or so, I meet someone new whom I find absolutely fascinating and want to know better. These people come from diverse cultures and socio-economic backgrounds, and they are all fabulous. Your final mission this week is to identify one such person in your world. Single out one person who is on the sidelines of your life who you would like to get to know better. This person could be a distant family member such as a cousin or an in-law. Maybe it is a neighbor, or a salesperson you work with, a parent of one of your children's friends, a fellow student, someone who works in your company, or a person at the gym.

Go slow at first; you need to feel her out to be sure the friendship is a good fit and that she is receptive to a new friend in her life. You could begin by asking where she is from, or what hobbies she has or if she has been to a certain restaurant or movie. What you ask depends on how you and she met. If she is a parent, kids are always a good topic. If you met her at the gym, you might ask about sports she participates in, or you could ask about her background or work interests.

The first person you choose might turn out not to have as much in common with you as you initially thought. That's okay, you've gotten to know a new friend a little better and it is possible that the contact could enrich your life greatly in years to come. Just choose another person and see if their interests are more in line with yours. Eventually you will find a person you feel like you've known forever. When that happens, your life instantly becomes more rewarding as you reach out and get to know this new person. True friendship does not grow in a day or a week, obviously, but seeds can be planted that just might grow to last a lifetime.

Complete this exercise several times throughout the year. In a few years you will have a diverse network of strong and rewarding friendships to draw from, and possibly share some of the best experiences and memories of your life.

Week 22 Success Plan

* Identify your closest friends
* Do something nice and unexpected for an old friend
* Cultivate a new friend from those you know casually
* Repeat quarterly, or annually
* Get ready for fabulous and rewarding relationships

Week 23

DO YOU HEAR WHAT I HEAR?

"To listen is an effort, and just to hear is no merit. A duck hears also." —Igor Stravinsky

Have you ever had a conversation with someone and later the other person has a completely different take on what each of you said? That happens with my son and me all the time and I'm often thinking, "Where was I during this conversation?" The fact is, one of us was distracted and our inattention caused us to recall what we think we heard, rather than what was actually said.

People tune others out all the time, and the people most often tuned out are the ones who are closest to us—our family and friends. For example: did you really listen to what your spouse had to say this morning? Did you really take time to hear him—this man you vowed to love and honor and cherish above all others—did you really listen to him?

When was the last time you listened closely to what happened during your son's day at school? Were you thinking of an office conflict when your son was talking? And what about your boss, were you really listening to the new proposals for company policy, or did you tune her out, too?

In this era of multitasking, you probably do two or three or five activities at once. In order to focus, you need to stop doing everything simultaneously and concentrate on just one or two things at a time. When you listen to your children or your family or your friends, stop what you are doing and really listen. Nothing should be more important in life than those people who are in your inner circle, so when you listen, honor them by really listening.

Unfortunately, while most of us hear what people have to say, we have never learned to listen to what they are saying. The next time a person who is important in your life talks to you, stop what you are doing. Just stop. Clear your mind of all the clutter that is bouncing around in your brain, and look at her. This is a person who is a significant figure in your life, and she deserves the benefit of your undivided attention.

As you look, take notice of her facial expressions. Is she happy, sad, worried, or confused? Look at her posture. Is she tense, relaxed, confident, angry? Notice the state of her hair and her clothes. Really look, and recognize all of the visual cues she is giving you, remembering that ninety percent of communication is non-verbal.

Now listen to her voice, not what she is saying, but how she is saying it. Is the tone whiny, aggressive, or sad? Is her voice frightened, teasing, or maybe jubilant? Does she sound loud, soft, harsh or shrill?

Finally, only after you have listened between the words, listen to the words themselves. Understand that you aren't fully listening unless you are focusing, looking, and hearing. Just think of all the additional information you receive when you focus on someone. The words actually register in your brain rather than flying in one ear and out the other. If you focus, you will process the information more quickly and more efficiently. If you are truly looking at her while she speaks, you are also receiving many other pieces of information that help you understand her state of mind and offer clarity to her words. With this information, you will have a better idea of the real meaning behind the words.

One of the biggest problems we all have is a lack of communication skills; it's a skill in which we all can improve. Most of the fights between families and friends are really just a lack of communication—a lack of understanding. By listening (which includes focusing and looking), versus hearing, you have much more information in which to understand the other person and make suitable responses and decisions. If you listen rather than just hear, it is very possible that the words will take on a completely different meaning, and it should be a meaning that is much closer to their original intent than your interpretation of it when you just hear.

Just think of the closer understanding you will have of those around you when you stop to listen. Not hear, but listen. Your levels of communication will increase and your relationships will become more fulfilling. Here are a few ideas to point you in the right direction.

Step 1: Stop and Listen to Your Surroundings

We all become so accustomed to the background noises of our lives that we often do not consciously hear them. Take time this week as you move through your day to stop and listen to where you are. When you wake up in the morning, what do you hear? Are there birds singing? Are there sirens, or are there sounds of children laughing? Do you hear the coffee pot click on? Is there noise from a radio, or can you hear the neighbor's car door slam? Take note of all that you hear.

As you move to new locations, or as the day progresses, listen to the changes in the sounds around you. I live across the street from an elementary school, so I can hear the squeal of the bus brakes in the morning as the students are dropped off. Later, I hear the sounds of children when they are outside in formal gym class, or at recess—and these sounds are very different! I hear the sounds in the middle of the afternoon of traffic slowing on the street as parents line up to pick up their children. And I hear the silence of the school in the clear night air, sometimes punctuated with the bang of a door as a janitor goes in or out.

Step 2: Take a Listening Tour

Take a day this week and go somewhere you do not usually go. It might be to a park for lunch, or a walk in the woods, or a trip downtown. The tour could last an hour, a day, or an entire weekend. Find a comfortable place to sit and just listen. Take a few deep breaths, relax, clear your mind and focus solely on the sounds that you hear. Close your eyes and listen. What do you hear? Decide how these sounds differ from those you usually hear. Are there any sounds you cannot identify? Now open your eyes. Do you still hear the same sounds in the same way, or have the sounds changed? It might be fun to take a friend with you on your little tour. What your companion hears could be completely different from what you hear, and that alone makes for interesting discussion.

If you can't get away, try opening a window and experiencing the different sounds without the distortion of glass. Be creative in your environment and experiment with different ways to hear the same sounds.

Step 3: Listen to Others

There is probably someone in your life that you wish you were closer to. This week make a project of focusing on him when he speaks, and really listen to what is being said. Look at him, see his body language, watch his facial expressions. He should notice that you are paying more attention, and that tells him he is important to you. Knowing he is important to you and that you are really listening to what he has to say validates the relationship. With validation comes understanding, and great conversations where you really, truly listen to each other.

Week 23 Success Plan

* Listen to your surroundings wherever you go, and throughout the day
* Take a special listening tour and listen to different areas
* Listen with your eyes open, and also with your eyes closed
* Commit to doing a better job of listening to one specific person

TRUST SOMEONE

"One must be fond of people and trust them if one is not to make a mess of life." —E.M. Forster

As young children, we all depend on others to care for us, to see that we receive basic needs such as food, clothing and shelter. We trust pretty blindly that these needs will be met. But inevitably the day comes where we trust a parent to do something and she fails us. And as we mature, people will fail us more and more often until we sometimes reach the point where we do not trust anyone.

No one goes through life without being hurt or betrayed by someone they have trusted. Some people are hurt more—and more often—than others. But it is counterproductive to go through life not trusting anyone at all. To get the most out of life, we need the help and support of a strong team around us. Without that, we are missing out on a lot of what life has to offer. The key is in knowing whom to trust and how much.

To successfully trust others you have to understand one thing: trust has nothing to do with you and everything to do with the other person. Trust is an ongoing test of the responsibility and abilities of another person. It is a fine measure of their honor, their morals, and their integrity. It is not about you.

There are many levels of trust. On a lower level you might send your teen to the grocery store with twenty dollars and a list. You trust that she will accomplish several tasks with this: she will drive and arrive safely, she will actually find and get the items on the list, and she will return home in a timely manner with a receipt and your change. You also trust that she isn't hot-rodding all over town in your car and spending your twenty at the mall with her friends.

It's a small task, going to the grocery store, but it involves a certain level of trust, especially for a teenager. Whether or not this little mission is accomplished has nothing to do with you. Your teen will either do it, proving that your trust was well placed, or she won't. There are few things we can control in life and other people's actions are not among them. The importance of trust is that in giving it you are helping another to grow in responsibility.

On a higher level, we trust that certain people will not betray our confidences, that others will be there for us during hard times, and that special people will support us through thick and thin. We trust that spouses will be faithful, and that friends will feed the cat while we are away. The stakes are higher because if these events do not happen, the consequences to us are greater and we will feel a deeper hurt.

It's a sad fact that you will find very few people who will hold your trust close. Many will betray your trust, so it becomes doubly important that you develop a method for determining whom to and whom not to trust—and with what.

Keep in mind that just because one person hurt you, not everyone will. Every person is an individual, and you cannot judge one person by the actions of another. You'll never know if you can trust a specific person unless you give him the opportunity to prove himself. To determine if someone in your life is worthy of your trust, give him a little and see what he does with it.

When my son was five he loved to chew gum, but he was not responsible enough to dispose of it properly. I'd find wads of it under tables, on toys, and even in the carpet. So I stopped the gum chewing. I could not trust Colby to be responsible with his used gum and told him we'd try again when he was six. Well, his sixth birthday rolled around and with it a pack of gum. I couldn't watch him every second, in fact it was not my job to be sure he threw his used gum in the trash. Colby needed to learn to be responsible enough so he could be trusted to do what was right and throw his gum away. I found that at six, he still wasn't quite there. But at age seven, we tried again and there has not been a problem, with gum anyway, since.

The trust I gave to Colby was not about me. I had to trust Colby enough to give him the opportunity to succeed or fail on his own.

Step 1: Give a Little Trust

This week commit to trusting others in small ways by giving them small tasks to accomplish or, especially with children, small gains in privileges. Trust your instincts as to what level of trust the individual can hold. Then step back and watch what happens. Certainly you hope the person will prove himself worthy of your trust, but know that it is quite possible that he won't. And that's okay. Instead of feeling hurt, choose to feel mildly disappointed in him instead. Think of it as an exercise in growth, both for you and the person you trusted.

If the person you chose held your trust favorably, that is wonderful! As he gains your trust he will also grow in responsibility and integrity, which will be an amazing process for you to watch. You can now give him a little more and if he does well, then you can give a little more after that. Eventually you will find to what level you can trust certain people. Most people have an invisible trust threshold above which they cannot be trusted. With some people that threshold is very high, and with others it is very low.

If your assistant proves she cannot be trusted with a specific task or piece of information, try to determine why. Was it something inherent in her nature and she cannot be trusted in this area? Or was it too much to ask of her at that time? If that's the case, try again with something that requires a smaller level of trust and see how it goes.

The reason so many others hurt us, is that we give too much trust too soon. Either she is not ready for it or we have not known her long enough—or well enough—or we have not realized yet that she is an untrustworthy person. By building trust in small steady increments, people may surprise or disappoint us, but they don't hurt us, or not nearly as badly.

You may find that there are some people whom you can trust to rush to your aid in times of crisis, but you cannot trust them with confidences, or vice versa. You'll find that you have to set limits on your relationship. That's okay, too. All people cannot be all things, but by understanding what you can and cannot trust, and with which people, your relationships will become stronger. You know where the boundaries are and as long as you stay within those boundaries, you can learn from and create great memories with this person. Step outside what you know to be a trust boundary, however, and you immediately run into problems.

This week, see how many different people you can find to trust with responsibilities both small and large. They may just surprise you by stepping up to the plate and surpassing your wildest expectations.

Step 2: Build Trust in Yourself

When I first moved to Nashville, I didn't know a soul. But I found immediate acceptance simply because I did what I said I would do. People developed a level of trust that I would deliver on my promises, and my business grew. In actuality, I stepped outside my skill level and really scrambled to make some of those promises a reality, because gaining my clients' trust was so important to me.

This week you will search out opportunities to prove your trustworthiness to those around you. But before you can do that, you need to know how much you can trust yourself. The following are areas in which people's trust can easily be misplaced, so take a moment to evaluate your trustworthiness in each of these areas:

Love. Are you faithful to promises you make to loved ones?
Money. Can you be trusted to handle money responsibly?
Business. Are you honorable in business deals? Do you make sure you offer fair terms in contracts and negotiations?
Friendship. Can your friends count on you to follow through with things you agree to? Can they trust you to hold confidences?

Once you have evaluated your level of trust, you can seek out opportunities to prove your trustworthiness to others. For example, if your boss is asking for volunteers at work for a specific project, jump on it. Or better yet, seek out extra tasks you can do on your own. Really go the extra mile with family and friends and deliver, as you never have before. Be positive, though, that you be will able to handle whatever you get yourself into. Use realistic assessments of your abilities and time commitments and do not take on more than you can manage.

Here are a few specific ideas to help you along. If you know you could do a better job of handling money, commit to doing a fabulous job with your funds for a week or a month. Your family will be pleasantly surprised and will also appreciate your efforts. If you cannot be trusted to arrive on time, commit to adding fifteen minutes to your travel time so you arrive right on the dot.

You know the areas in which you fail those around you—we all have some. Choose one area and make an effort like you never have before to prove that you can be trusted in that specific area. Then as soon as you have that problem licked, find another area. It will take some time. Habits do not die overnight, nor are skills developed instantly. But you will notice that as soon as you prove yourself in one area, people will begin trusting you in other areas as well. By the time your level of trust reaches it's highest point, you will have realized some astounding changes in your relationships with those around you.

* Give a little trust to those around you
* Step back and watch how they handle it
* Raise or lower your trust expectations of them based on their performance
* Seek opportunities to prove yourself trustworthy

DO A GOOD DEED DAILY

"Neither fire nor wind, birth nor death can erase our good deeds."
—Buddha

Everyone has seen pictures of the Boy Scout helping the old lady across the street. This week you get to be an honorary Boy Scout as you go out of your way to help people you normally would not help. You will have as much fun as the boy scouts do, when you do a good deed daily.

There is great satisfaction in assisting others, and every day brings new and unexpected opportunities to lend a helping hand. A few winters ago country-rocker Ricky Lynn Gregg, who was a client at the time, was touring in South Dakota. As his tour bus was making its way to the Native American venue where he was to perform, he saw the strange sight of people sawing off pieces of their frame houses. After he did his sound check, he asked a local resident about what he had seen. Ricky was shocked by the answer.

"People were sawing off wood from their homes because they were cold and needed firewood," said Ricky. "I couldn't believe people were that poor—that we had those kinds of conditions right here in the United States."

Instead of just being appalled, Ricky decided to do something. He organized a charitable event called the Trail of Hope and over the next year and a half he and a small committee organized, gathered, and delivered six semi-truckloads of donated clothes and supplies to twelve Native American communities. Both my son and I were privileged to be part of the Trail of Hope, and helped unload several of those trucks in near-blizzard conditions.

It was a wonderful experience, but the icing on the cake was a phone call I received a week or so after we got back. A social worker at one of the communities told me that they had split up our donations—which included books, toiletries, clothes, toys, medicines and other goods—into over six hundred care packages. She had called specifically to tell me that one six-year-old girl began to cry with joy when she found a toothbrush in her package. This little Native American girl could not believe that this toothbrush was her very own. In her entire life, no one in her family had ever owned a toothbrush.

The good deed that you do every day need not involve months of planning, committees, and semi-trucks driving thousands of miles. Making a difference in someone's life is very simple. Your good deed might be helping a neighbor trim trees, or picking up something a stranger dropped—rather than just walking on by. It could be offering to run an errand, or opening a door for an older person. You could carry packages, cook a meal, water plants, hold an elevator, walk a dog, pick up trash, or a bazillion-and-one other things.

One winter I took David Allan Coe to New York to shoot a television pilot. We had a little extra time at the end of the day and he wanted to go to the Diamond District to see if he could find a ring in the shape of a piano. To get a true visual picture you have to know that David is a powerfully built man who stands over six feet tall. On this day he had waist-length blonde hair, a beard braided and adorned with beads, numerous tattoos and was what I can only describe as "exotically dressed." There we were David, a bodyguard, and me, looking in one glittering window after the next with the stretch limo trailing behind. Between shops, and next to an alley, we passed an elderly homeless man sitting on a thin piece of cardboard over a sewer grate. The man had no legs.

"Hey," the man called to David. "Ain't you Johnny Cash?"

Before David could answer, the homeless man continued, "Sure you are, I'd know you anywhere," and he began to sing a verse of the Johnny Cash hit, "I Walk the Line."

Now for most of his life Johnny Cash had black hair. I cannot ever recall a time when it was blonde, or even shoulder-length, much less waist-length. Cash was always clean-shaven and if he ever had a beard, he didn't strike me as the type to braid it, and certainly not with colorful beads. Yet this man was convinced that David was Johnny Cash.

"Why yes, I am," David told the man after a glance in my direction.

The two went on to have a ten-minute conversation about music, politics, sports, women and food. When he left David offered the man a hundred dollar bill, but the man said he wouldn't know what to do with so much money and would only accept five.

As we walked away, and before I could say a word, David said to me, "That man waited all his life to meet Johnny Cash. He obviously hasn't had much luck lately and he wanted so badly to believe I was Cash, that for a few minutes I was. Giving him a few moments of happiness was the least I could do."

David Allan Coe had done his good deed for the day, just by spending a little time with an old man who was sitting on a sewer grate. David didn't have to stop; he didn't have to talk or offer him anything. But David did because he not only knew it was the right thing to do, but because it made both the homeless man and he feel like a million bucks.

Step 1: Do a Good Deed Daily
This week you will have a great time as you go out of your way to help a person you ordinarily would not have helped. The beauty of this entire week is that there is nothing you can plan. Just be observant and watch for opportunities to help others as you go through your day.

As a writer, I do not come into physical contact with other people every single day. Sometimes I hole up for several days in front of my computer and that makes it hard to get out and help others. But when I do go out, I have a great time. I sometimes find I can help five people in just as many minutes. It's a fabulous cure for writer's block. All I have to do is be aware that situations arise all the time where I can help. Usually, it just takes a few seconds.

You also don't need to look for totally destitute people, such as those whom Ricky and David helped. Regular people need help too, and they are everywhere—at the store, library, post office, school, office, gym, and the park. If you open a door for a co-worker, that's a good deed. If papers fall out of someone else's folder and you stop to help pick them up, that's another good deed. Offering to get coffee or juice for a friend is another.

Step 2: Get Other People Involved

The possibilities are endless. Get a friend involved and see who can do the most good deeds in a week, a day, an hour or just ten minutes. Make it a family, classroom or club project and challenge other groups to exceed your total.

As you go through your week, you will feel better and better about yourself. You will gain confidence, and while it might be difficult to spot great opportunities to help at first, as you become more experienced they will pop out at you right and left.

Step 3: Keep Tabs

This week in your *Success Within* notebook, keep a list of all the different people and the ways in which you helped them. You'll be pretty amazed at yourself by week's end, guaranteed!

Week 25 Success Plan

* Every day, seek opportunities to help others
* Get friends and family involved and see who can help the most people
* Keep a list of everyone you helped and how you helped them

REPEAT AND REPEAT AGAIN

"Repeat anything often enough and it will start to become you."
—Tom Hopkins

Once again you are taken back over the last twelve weeks to reconsider and confirm. And, as before, it is your choice whether you move on to the next thirteen weeks, or return to individual steps or success plans.

It is hard to introduce new ideas into our lives. We all have certain ways of doing things that are so comfortable that we become happy in our own little world. But eventually that little world will become stagnant and the years will pass almost before you know it. That's why it is important to take steps now to enrich both your life and the lives of those closest to you. You owe it to the people you care about and to yourself. Remember that it will take time and commitment; you have to take action to make change happen. But almost everyone can find a few minutes a day to invest in the rest of his or her life.

Step 1: Assess Your Success Plans
This is a week for assessment, for appraisal and evaluation. It's an important week because in looking back, you will see just how far you have come and also begin to see just how far you have yet to go.

Let's do a quick review:

1. How many people were you able to "put up" in Week 14? How many since that week? Was this easy or difficult to incorporate into your life? Do you see yourself doing this long-term? Why or why not?

2. Were you able to forgive someone in Week 15? Who? Was it easier or harder than you thought to move on? What was the biggest lesson you learned from this experience? Do you think it will be easier for you to forgive others in the future? Why or why not?

3. In Week 16, what specific qualities did you find to respect about yourself? About those around you? What personality traits did you personally make an effort to change? Have you kept up with this effort? Why or why not?

4. Did Week 17 bring you closer to a person you cared about? How difficult was it to begin a conversation with them? Do you find it easier to talk or listen? What specific things did you learn about yourself, the other person, and your relationship?

5. What news item did you choose to analyze in Week 18? Why did you choose that specific item? How many different scenarios were you able to invent about the news event? Did this exercise make you see this news piece a little differently? How has this concept helped you in your personal life?

6. What negative words from Week 19 were the toughest to eliminate from your vocabulary? How hard did you initially have to think about positive speech patterns when you first began this, as compared to now? Did you

notice any difference in people you chose to prime with positive words? Have you made this exercise part of your daily life? Why or why not?

7. In Week 20, were you able to view unfair situations from another viewpoint? How easy was it for you to switch roles and why? If you used costumes or props, did they help you get into the role or relieve tension? What was the biggest lesson you learned from this exercise?

8. How many people could you find to give credit to in Week 21? Did you find people wanting to give you credit as well? What was the most unusual phrase that you came up with?

9. In Week 22 did your list of friends surprise you in any way? If so, how? What was the nicest act you could think of to do for an old friend? What was their reaction? Who did you find that you'd like to befriend?

10. Were you surprised by everything you heard in Week 23? Where did you go for your listening tour? What was most rewarding about that location? Was it very difficult for you to focus, look and listen? Has anyone you've been listening-better-to treated you any differently? If yes, how?

11. In Week 24, who around you really stepped up to earn your trust? Who let you down? How has evaluating the trustworthiness of friends and family members helped you? With what unique opportunities did you seek to show your trustworthiness to others?

12. How many people did you help in Week 25? How did you go out of your way to help? Describe how helping others made you feel. Were you able to convince any family members or friends to also help others? If so, as the week wore on, did you notice any change in them?

Week 26 Success Plan

★ Thoroughly assess weeks fourteen to twenty-five
★ Commit to evaluating two of the weeks every day
★ Decide what areas you should explore more fully, if any
★ Treat yourself to something nice for successfully completing this second section

3

IMPROVE YOURSELF

Each week in Part 2 deals with how well you treat other people. Here, you begin to reach out, and by treating others extraordinarily well you will find the extraordinary coming back to you. In the process, you will create some of life's greatest moments. You'll also see another exciting development begin to happen: the knowledge that you are suddenly doing better in many areas of your life. All of a sudden relationships, work life, and home life are coming together as never before. It's a simple thing. It's called success.

PLAN YOUR WORK
AND WORK YOUR PLAN

"Before beginning, plan carefully." —Marcus Tullius Cicero

When I was in high school, I played the flute and participated in regional and state competitions. But I didn't miraculously peak on the day of competition. I had to develop a carefully planned practice schedule, then execute it strategically. Every step had to be constantly reevaluated, plans had to be updated as I progressed, and factors such as the possibility of contracting a cold had to be considered. It was only careful execution of a detailed plan that delivered a strong sense of accomplishment.

The same goes for a book. A book doesn't become a bestseller without an intricate plan that involves sales, marketing, promotion, signings and speeches by the author, hundreds of phone calls, and major press. In other words, there is a detailed plan in place to create interest in the book.

Every project, every business, has to have a plan. My friend J. D. Haas facilitates trips that are tied to radio and television promotions. He takes groups of winners from individual radio and television stations on fantastic trips to Las Vegas for the Academy of Country Music Awards, to Hollywood for tapings of *Reba* and other sitcoms, to NASCAR races, and to many other exciting cities and events. Imagine "sheparding" four hundred people through three days in Las Vegas. Flights and hotels have to be booked, and ground transportation has to be arranged. Everyone has to get to certain events on time. People have to be fed, questions have to be answered, emergencies have to be handled, and most importantly, everyone has to have a great time. J.D.'s trips do not just happen. There are numerous minute details that have to be completed before the trip can be considered a success.

Many people just like you have all kinds of goals they'd like to accomplish. It could be learning to play a musical instrument, taking Spanish lessons, landscaping their yard, moving to a new home—the list is endless. Unfortunately, even though people talk about doing all of these wonderful things, most of their dreams never happen because unlike you, these people do not have a plan. Back in Week 2 we discussed the dreams, desires and goals formula—making colorful lists of events you'd like to happen in your life in order of the amount of effort it would take to make it happen. If Week 2 is not fresh in your memory, you may wish to skim it again now. (If you neglected to make your lists in Week 2, now is a really good time to choose a few items that "someday" you'd like to achieve.)

If you have made your lists and kept up with them, hopefully you have been able to cross some of your immediate goals off your goals-list, having replaced them with gold stars, exclamation points or other signs of success. This is also a good moment to reflect on your initial goals and desires lists to see how far you have (or haven't) come.

This week focuses on bringing one of the items on the middle list, the desires list, a little closer to reality. These are things that take more time and planning than cleaning out a closet, or calling your grandmother. It might be learning to snowboard, becoming debt free, writing a book, taking a big vacation, organizing a family reunion, or taking a business to another level.

Knowing that nothing happens unless you make it happen, it is still important to be realistic in your choices. Being realistic means having a good handle on your time commitments, your finances, and the other resources you will need to accomplish whatever it is that you want to do.

Step 1: Do it Now

This week it is a must that you devote a few minutes every day to making your dream a reality. Remember, if you don't do it, nothing will happen. Keep the wonderful time you will have and your great sense of impending accomplishment fresh in your mind, both as motivation for this week. So right now, today, choose something fairly big to work toward making a reality.

Once you have made your choice, personalize it. Take a moment to really think what it will be like to visit your college friends, or to learn to paint. Visualize the sights, sounds, and smells you will have during this wonderful experience.

Step 2: Develop a Plan

Now that you have chosen what you are going to do, you have to figure out how you are going to do it. List all the individual steps that will take you from where you are now to where you want to ultimately be. Be as detailed as possible. In writing this book, for instance, I needed to come up with the idea, research the market, make an outline, write a book proposal, flesh out several sample chapters, find an agent, agree to the publisher's terms, develop a daily writing schedule, and write a certain number of words every day to meet my deadline.

Step 3: Details, Details

This is where your plan really begins to take shape! For every step you listed in step 2, you now are ready to make a detailed and itemized plan. For example, to research the market for this book, I had to spend a lot of time on Amazon.com, bn.com and other major online book sites looking for books of similar subject matter. When I found them, I recorded all the details about the book: author, publisher, year published, size, number of pages, etc. I even read a lot of the books I researched. I also had to spend time in bookstores and libraries to see what style of writing worked best, and what formats were selling well. Additionally, I talked to a lot of people and asked them what they would like in a book such as this. I talked to friends, and to people who worked in libraries and bookstores. I talked to other authors, to neighbors, to people I knew very well, and to people I hardly knew. To make it fun, I kept a notebook with the results of all my research and my thoughts. I used brightly colored stickers in different shapes to quickly access specifics that I needed, as well as important reminders. I planned my work and worked my plan, and everything went along surprisingly well.

Step 4: Take Action

After you have listed all the steps to make your plan a reality, it is time to begin. Take the first item on your list and run with it. Remember that you only have to find small chunks of time to achieve forward movement. It is amazing what most people can accomplish in consistent increments of five or ten minutes if they really focus. If you are planning a vacation and are checking out various hotels, you might pull a list of all the hotels in the area, or check out one hotel at a time. You could even enlist the help of others who are going on the trip with you. Checking hotel prices and amenities is a great learning experience for a teenager, and frees up your time to do something else. Delegating is a fabulous way to get things done faster. Even if you are going on the trip by yourself, you may have friends who are eager to share the experience with you and want to help.

Remember that every little step you cross off your list is one big step closer to making something significant happen in your life. Depending on the project you choose—plus your time, funding, and other resources—it might take you a week or it might take you a year, but every action will be bringing you closer to your goal.

Week 27 Success Plan

* Choose something from your desires list to make a reality
* Personalize and visualize your success
* List the major steps you need to take
* Develop the details of each major step
* Make it fun
* Enlist help if possible
* Begin with one step at a time

Week 28

GET FIT

"Physical fitness is not only one of the most important keys to a healthy body, it is the basis of dynamic and creative intellectual activity." —John Fitzgerald Kennedy

Becoming physically fit is one area where most people really need some help. I'm not talking about a diet here, let's make that clear. I'm talking about increasing your level of physical activity and increasing your muscle tone so you feel better. Weight loss could be a nice side product of this, but it is not the main focus this week.

There are many reasons to be fit, the least of which is looking great. Those who are fit are healthier, have more stamina, are mentally sharper, and have fewer sick days. But most people don't like to exercise because it takes time they don't think they have. Let's face it, getting fit takes effort.

I once had a country music client who . . . well let's just say he needed to lose a significant amount of weight for a photo shoot. This artist was what we call a "baby act," meaning that he was new in the industry, and his record label told me that if he couldn't lose the weight—which he had gained after he was signed—his record deal would be in jeopardy.

This artist complained that while he was touring, there was no time to exercise, and that the hotels he stayed in didn't have work-out rooms. I suggested he run up and down the hotel stairs. He said security was an issue. I suggested he take someone with him when he ran. I asked him to invest a few dollars in a portable stair stepper. He said there wasn't enough room on the bus. When I reminded him that the portable models are about the size of two shoeboxes he said they didn't have time to stop anywhere to get one. I pointed out that other artists take portable basketball hoops with them, or bands made of rubber to help stretch and tone their bodies. Other artists make it a point to get off the bus early and jog for fifteen minutes on a minitrampoline or around the block, but he just couldn't see the need or find the time. On and on it went, one excuse after another. The end result: the artist lost his record deal and hasn't really been heard from since.

Essentially, we are a lazy, obese society. We choose the closest parking space to the store instead of one further away, even though walking from the further spot is healthier. We sit in front of the television instead of cleaning up the yard, we take the elevator instead of the stairs, and we opt-out of a lot of fun activities because they take too much effort. In exchange, we live lives compromised by our physical limitations and die a lot younger than we need to.

Everyone has his or her own level of capability when it comes to being physically fit. You cannot compare a fitness plan for a twelve-year-old boy to that of a sixty-year-old woman. Nor can you compare the level of physical activity for a healthy woman in her twenties to that of a wheelchair-bound paraplegic, just as you cannot compare the potential ability of a middle-aged man with high cholesterol and diabetes to a former professional athlete with Multiple Sclerosis. It is all relative. The point is to push yourself to do just as much as *you* can possibly do, which is most likely more than what you are doing now.

A while back I had a freak accident where I hopped off the back of my truck, tore a ligament in my knee and broke my leg. This is the same knee that was injured in a fall years ago that ended my professional riding career. This time I was in a wheelchair for a month both pre- and post-surgery, and on crutches or walking with a cane for several months afterward. Then I developed scar tissue requiring additional surgery. All in all, I was laid up for almost a year. My physical activity during that time was obviously not at the level it was before the accident. But I did the best that I could during that time and still have some well-developed arm muscles to prove it.

When I was training horses and riding eight of them every day, staying fit was not a problem. But for those who have desk jobs or who stand on their feet all day, staying physically fit can be far more difficult. That is why it is important to make it fun. I hate jogging and my orthopedist has cautioned that it is not good for my knees. So instead, twice a week I ride horses. I wear a pedometer and try to take 10,000 steps every day, which is a fairly ambitious number for me. Twice a week I work out with a set of three-pound dumbbells. I do toning exercises with long, thin strips of rubber. I garden, I walk, and when I have the opportunity, I swim. If I was told the only way I could exercise is to jog, I'd never do it, because it is not something I enjoy.

We all have our own set of health concerns and injuries that prevent us from a specific activity. Each of us also has a myriad of likes and dislikes that lead us toward one activity or another. Additionally, work and family commitments dictate how much time we have for all the rest of the activities we need to fit into our lives, including exercise.

Sometimes you have to get creative to make it all work. When my son was younger and was playing baseball, I obviously wanted to watch all his practices, but it was also the only time I could find to exercise. The perfect solution was joining a group of parents who walked around the ball field. That way we could enjoy watching our kids and exercise at the same time. It is always nice when you can accomplish two things simultaneously.

On days when I am writing I tend to stay at the computer far too long, so every hour I take a five-minute break and skip around the house, or do jumping jacks. When I go downstairs to let the dog out, I practice walking backwards up the steps—without touching the hand-rails. I spend five minutes on the treadmill. I watch very little television, but when I do, I make sure to get up and jog in place during the commercials, or do stretching exercises during the program. So even if I cannot find a spare hour in my day to go to the gym—which I would never do anyway—throughout the day I am getting quite a bit of exercise.

Whenever I feel like not exercising, I remember my friend Loretta Johnson. Loretta and her sisters, Loudilla and Kay, co-founded the International Fan Club Organization and over the past thirty years have been instrumental in the careers of over a hundred music stars. Loretta has been diagnosed with bone marrow cancer and an immune/neurological condition called chronic inflammatory demyelinating polyneuropathy. Loretta is one of only a handful of people in the world who has this very rare combination of illnesses. She has also been paralyzed several times and suffered a back fracture while in the hospital for medical treatment. Whenever I feel like slacking off, I remember that Loretta gets up at five A.M. every morning to walk three miles on her treadmill.

This week you will commit to increasing the physical activity in your life and find fun ways to do it. You have a lot of wonderful moments ahead of you and if you are physically fit, you will enjoy them all the more.

Step 1: Find a Fun Activity

Make a personal commitment to yourself to increase your level of activity. To do this you have to find some activities that you enjoy that also fit in with the rest of your schedule.

If you are not sure what kinds of activities you like, make this a week for experimenting. Try walking in a park, or going to a gym. Just because I do not like gyms doesn't mean it isn't a perfect fit for you. Go bowling, or go to a playground and swing on the swings.

You can perform activities around the house that involve exercise as well. Shovel some snow, trim the bushes, mow the lawn with a push mower. If you don't have a yard, volunteer to help an elderly neighbor or relative rake leaves and you too will be accomplishing two things at once—you will be helping someone and exercising all at the same time.

If you are able, try something new like racquetball, basketball, tennis, canoeing or golf. If not, throw a lightweight ball against a wall and catch it. I know from experience that this can be done while sitting in a wheelchair or lying on the couch. If your level of fitness is pretty low, do some hand stretching exercises, or shoulder rolls. You could even play with a slinky or get one of those paddles with a ping-pong ball attached to a string.

Remember that every single step you take, every additional movement you make brings your level of fitness to a higher level. The idea is to take your current level of physical activity and increase it. And, it doesn't have to be boring. Find something you like to do, and then do it.

If you already have activities that you enjoy, increase the level. If you walk, try walking further than usual, or carrying a light set of dumb bells, or wearing a backpack with a few canned goods in it to add weight. At work, spend five minutes going up and down the stairs during your lunch period or get a few people together to walk around the block. Do arm circles as you dust, move heavy objects as you clean out the garage, put on some music and do the twist. Better yet, host a regular Friday-night Twist Party.

Commit this week to some increase in your level of physical activity every single day.

Step 2: Watch What You Eat

Although this is not "diet and weight loss week," it is worth taking the time to evaluate what you eat. Sometimes very small changes can make a huge difference in how you feel. And if you feel better, you will move around more. So evaluate your diet, and find out the best combination of foods to make you feel your absolute best.

Week 28 Success Plan

* Increase your level of physical activity
* Find fun activities to do that get you moving
* Do them regularly
* Evaluate what you eat so you feel your absolute best

Week 29

GET OUT OF DEBT

"When there is no cash left, you stop spending. It's as simple as that, and it works." —Dave Ramsey

If you listen to Dave Ramsey's syndicated radio show, *The Dave Ramsey Show*, you'll learn that cash is king and debt is dumb. I believe in that message so much that I could just say listen to Dave's show and be done with it.

People who have a lot of cash and little debt are not necessarily more successful than the next person—you are not a success if you are without debt and still a jerk. But people who have a high cash/low debt ratio have less stress in their lives, and financial stress can debilitate both your health and your relationships. If you live on less than you make, give yourself a huge round of applause, for you are the exception to the rule, and that means you are exceptional! Congratulations.

The amount of money you have—or don't have—doesn't really matter as long as you have enough to meet your basic needs, plus a little left over to invest in your future. I know people who have no debt and are saving money on thirty thousand a year, and others who are in debt up to their eyeballs at three hundred thousand dollars a year. Just because someone is making big bucks doesn't mean they are spending them wisely.

Most people who have a sizable amount of cash stashed away don't have as much debt proportionate to their incomes as other people because they live within their means and they pay cash. When was the last time you figured out what you were really paying for your car? If the sticker price was around fifteen thousand, with zero down and sixty payments you paid well over that. The difference is that those who paid cash will have extra money to pay off their mortgage or invest for their retirement because they are not paying interest. That's how the rich keep getting richer and the poor poorer.

If you are over fifty, chances are your grandparents paid cash for everything and lived a life of dignity in their later years. Many of today's elderly are struggling to pay debts they incurred twenty years ago. Have you ever stopped to think how will you spend your later years? Will you be traveling to exotic places, or flat broke and living in a nursing home? If you stay in debt with car and credit card payments, student loans, and a second mortgage, the latter is the most likely scenario for you. It doesn't matter how young or old you are, every step you take toward debt reduction is saving you money.

I mentioned earlier that debt is stressful. I can personally attest that it is very difficult to enjoy the fruits of life when you are stressing over the electricity being turned off. Debt will strangle you in many ways—financially, obviously—but also emotionally, physically, and mentally. Every area of your life will suffer if you are spending more than you make.

We all know that life is full of unexpected twists and turns. I have known more than a few recording artists who were thrown into bankruptcy when they lost their record deals. All of a sudden their records are pulled from the shelves of the stores. Without product to sell and without a deal, radio play diminishes. When airplay goes down, the dollar amount the artist can pull every night from tour dates dwindles. All of a sudden the artists are making half of what they used to, yet they still have the high costs of the bus, the band, the mansion, the publicist, and everything else a career entails.

Other artists like Shenandoah and Joe Diffie have been devastated financially when they have had unexpected legal battles over the trademark of a name or the copyright of a song. I know of a horse breeder who was put out of business when his top stallion—who was uninsured—was struck by lightning and killed. No matter who you are or what you do, disasters happen. People get sick or lose their jobs. Couples divorce. Companies close. A steady stream of income can be turned off in an instant, and most people are not prepared.

This week could be one of the most important weeks in your life. Imagine living a debt free, stress free life. Imagine having a solid financial future, and knowing that your twilight years will be spent enjoying all that life has to offer. The best part of all? You don't have to win the lottery or earn a million dollars a year to have all that. You can take the first steps toward enjoying your new financial future simply by doing the following.

Step 1: Read and Listen Your Way Out of Debt
If you haven't done so already, for the sake of your future and the well-being of your family, begin working toward living a debt free lifestyle. You owe it to yourself and to them. For most, it will not happen overnight. There are usually more than a few bad habits to change and unless you just

found a "few million" lying around in the attic, it takes time to change the financial flow from debt to wealth. To help you learn to live debt free, listen to the daily syndicated radio program, *The Dave Ramsey Show*. If it is not broadcast in your area, or if you can't tune in at work, you can listen online anytime at daveramsey.com. If you're not online, then get one of his books—he has written several. This will be one of the best investments of your time that you will make in your entire life.

Step 2: Get on a Budget and Stay There

Everyone has a budget. Yours could be two thousand dollars a month or two million. It doesn't matter how much you have or don't have, you need to plan how to spend your money, or before you know, it will be gone. Begin by listing every possible monthly expense that you can think of at the beginning of every month. Be sure to include money you spend on fast food, entertainment, double mocha lattes, credit card bills, school fees, and money you hand out to your kids. Then look at the income you have that month. If your expenses are more than your income, you'll either have to cut back somewhere or find a way to earn more money. If the difference is sizable, you'll need to take serious measures, such as selling extra furniture, having the cable turned off, selling a car, or getting a second job. If you don't act now, every month you will be digging a deeper financial hole. Eventually, you *will* fall in.

Step 3: Recruit the Support of Your Family and Friends

Making such a big change in your life will require the support of your friends, and especially your family. Those you live with will have to be on board or you will be fighting a losing battle. You can stem the flow somewhat by yourself, but you need help to repair the dam. Some people will need to ease into the idea, others will become as excited as you are and want to jump right in. Whatever the situation, know that every effort you make is a step in the right direction.

Week 29 Success Plan

* Commit to a debt free life
* Learn more by reading or listening to Dave Ramsey
* Do a monthly budget every month
* Take drastic measures, if necessary
* Enlist support from friends and family
* Hang in there
* Enjoy the security of financial freedom

HELPING OTHERS HELPS YOU

"We cannot build our own future without helping others to build theirs." —Bill Clinton

One of the greatest joys of being a publicist has been being involved in all the charitable work my clients do. Over the years I've gotten to know and work with many wonderful people whom I otherwise never would have met. I have also gotten to see the difference that has resulted in the lives of those who need help the most

Rick Stevens is a very talented vocalist from Bakersfield who has a daughter with severe asthma. When he expressed interest in helping other kids with asthma, I called the American Lung Association. Almost before I knew it Rick was the spokesperson for the American Lung Association's Children's Asthma Camps. One summer Rick visited several of the camps, gave concerts and encouraged the kids to follow their dreams. Afterward, several of the camp directors forwarded very positive feedback to me and I felt very proud that my small contribution to this effort gave so many kids support.

I understood the importance of charitable works for my clients because I grew up in a home that valued volunteerism. When I was young, my mom was room mother, then president of the PTA. She was on the park commission, the mental health commission, and the school board. She advocated for bike/hike paths along the roads in our community, gave speeches to the rose society, and eventually became executive director of the Servicemen's Center at the Minneapolis/St. Paul Airport where she coordinated schedules of over two hundred volunteers. She volunteered because she had an interest in certain areas and felt she had something to offer.

It was a given as I grew older that I, too, would volunteer to help with events that I was interested in and in areas where I felt I could help. After my son was born I became a Cub Scout leader. As a publicist I became involved in programs to keep guns out of schools, programs that offered assistance to victims, groups that gave help to Native Americans, and causes that promoted awareness of diabetes and the hearing impaired. My work in those areas was, by far, the most rewarding of my professional life.

It's a fact: helping others helps you. You have a joyous feeling inside when you see a smile on the face of those you have helped. There are many avenues of volunteerism and each in its own way can bring joy, friendship, encouragement, hope and much, much more. Volunteering an hour a month, once a week, or several hours a day, if your schedule allows, helps those in need more than most will ever know. It also helps you feel needed and worthy, and those are all wonderful feelings.

Owen Beck is a young heavyweight fighter who at the time of this writing is 24-1 and is ranked fourth in the world. He loves being in the boxing ring but his passion is motivating kids. Whenever he can, he talks to groups of kids about his own disadvantaged childhood in Jamaica, and how staying positive and focusing on a dream can turn a life around. Owen is a willing role model who has found his greatest joy in helping others.

I currently am a volunteer at Saddle Up!, a therapeutic horseback riding program for disabled children in middle Tennessee. It is perfect for me because it combines horses and children, which are two of my strongest interests. Here, as in other volunteer programs, there are many great moments—very special one-on-ones with others who depend on a volunteer's help and support.

One of my most memorable experiences is helping three nine-year-old Down's syndrome boys give a horse a bath. Once they got over their awe of the water coming out of the hose, they were fascinated by the way the water parted the horse's hair and the feel of a wet brush versus a dry one. They then took turns peering into the water drain and exclaiming at the interesting sound the water made as it ran into the hole. I'm not sure how clean the horse got, but we all had a lot of fun.

Another great moment involved the first word an autistic child had ever spoken—when he said "hi" to his horse. To me, those moments are everything. They mean far more than being backstage at a big awards show, or winning world championships with a horse or rider, because I'm right there and can see that I made a positive difference.

There are many different ways to volunteer—alone or in a group, and within a wide variety of interests. A singles group could pick up litter from a stretch of highway once a month, or adopt a grandparent. An individual could participate in a local neighborhood watch program, deliver meals, or teach someone to read. Volunteering also is a great way to meet people and make new friends.

Former United States President Jimmy Carter (Habitat for Humanity), pop star Clay Aiken (UNICEF), singer

Kevin Sharp (Make-A-Wish-Foundation), and many other celebrities have spoken positively about their volunteer experiences and of the lasting friendships they have made through their efforts. And, as a cancer survivor, Kevin Sharp knows first hand how much the efforts of volunteers can mean. He credits the wish he received through the Make-A-Wish-Foundation as being instrumental in his recovery from cancer.

While still in high school, Kevin began experiencing pain and fatigue that was later diagnosed as a rare form of bone cancer. As a high school senior, Kevin was given the devastating news that his chance of survival was slim. Uncertain if he would even live six months, Kevin was introduced to the Make–A–Wish–Foundation, which grants wishes to children with life-threatening illnesses. The foundation honored Kevin's wish of meeting producer / performer David Foster, whose friendship sustained Kevin through two years of intense chemotherapy, radiation treatments, and experimental drugs. David also opened a door for Kevin to pursue his dream of becoming a star.

Kevin went into remission in 1990 and has never forgotten the generosity of the Make-A-Wish-Foundation. He currently acts as a national spokesperson and has been honored with their prestigious Wishgranter of the Year Award. Kevin is, to date, the only wish child to become the wish request of other wish kids. The foundation gave to Kevin, now Kevin is giving back to them.

This week you too will be able to see the powerful benefits of volunteerism. You will feel very special as you either jump into a volunteer project of your own, or recommit to an existing effort.

Step 1: Find a Cause

There must be something you have a special interest in. Maybe it is reading, animal rights, skateboarding, AIDS, or the environment. Know that for every interest there is a group of people trying to help. If you love reading, you could volunteer to read to the blind or to people in the hospital or to kids at the library. This week take time to think about your special interests and find a volunteer group in your area that supports your interest. Some groups may be listed in the phone book, others may be a little more difficult to track down, but it should only take a call or two to find a contact who knows someone who knows someone. If you already have a volunteer commitment, shake it up a little. Become involved in a new project or develop a fundraising idea for the group to consider.

Step 2: Step Up to the Plate

When you find your group, commit to a specific time investment. Some people volunteer on a daily basis, others on a monthly basis, others just a few times a year. Volunteering doesn't have to consume all of your time. In every volunteer organization, there is something for everyone to do. At Saddle Up! the grounds committee keeps the place looking fabulous, the chuck wagon committee feeds the volunteers during special events, and the public relations committee helps bring awareness to the general public. Even if people don't have a specific interest in kids with disabilities or experience with horses, their assistance is needed and welcomed. In any group, there are web sites to design and newsletters to write, phone calls to make and emails to send, training programs to develop and fundraisers or other events to coordinate. In addition to helping a great cause, you will meet a lot of people who have the same interests as you and you will make some wonderful friends.

Week 30 Success Plan

* Find a cause or recommit to an existing organization
* Commit to a certain amount of time
* Request an area of responsibility
* Reap the many rewards of helping others

Week 31

RE-COMMIT TO SOMETHING

"There's no abiding success without commitment."
—Anthony Robbins

Everyone misses certain parts of their past. Maybe it's a friendship you remember fondly, or a sport you loved playing. It could be a talent—such as playing an instrument or painting—that for whatever reason is no longer an active part of you. Somehow life got in the way and this beautiful thing fell by the wayside. You might not even have realized it until it was too late

But is it ever too late? If you really miss something that was once important to you, all it takes is a new commitment to make it important once again. Finding something from the past and reincorporating it into your life today is not only a wonderful way for you to reconnect with some great moments in your life, it also gives you a nice sense of comfort and familiarity.

When I was a child, I loved horses so much that I went to college to study to be a horse trainer. But then life began leading me in other directions. When the horse I'd had since I was twelve died after twenty-three years as a member of my family, it was the beginning of a decade-long period of absence from the horses I loved so much.

For several years I fought it, for several more years I actually forgot about it, and then it took me a few more years to find my way back. You can't always revisit the past as it once was (I could not physically withstand the demands of riding full-time anymore). But I found there were other ways to incorporate horses into my life. I wrote a book about celebrities and their horses called *The Power of Horses*. The book flung open many doors for me, and when I found a local program that helped children with disabilities learn to ride, I knew I'd found a new home. I was once again riding, training, and teaching—this time part-time and not for the show ring, but to help handicapped children. Bringing horses back into my life enhances my days with a sense of familiarity and completion that was missing before. My decision to re-commit part of my time and attention to horses has been one of the best decisions of my life.

Every year along with champagne and the traditional New Year's Eve count down, some 100 million Americans make at least one New Year's resolution—a specific commitment to make the coming year better for themselves in some detailed way. I always resolve to improve one thing about myself (like learning to write phone numbers and messages in one place, rather than on little scraps of paper all over the house), and one thing that will help others (such as being a better neighbor).

According to a recent University of Washington survey, some people make their New Year's resolutions as early as May, others as late as late January, and most who make a resolution make more than one. Unfortunately, the study also found that after sixty days only 63 percent were still working toward their resolution, and of who successfully achieved their number one resolution, only 40 percent did so on the first try. The rest made multiple attempts, with 17 percent finally succeeding after more than six tries. So when it comes to resolutions or recommitment, if at first you don't succeed, try, try again. Perseverance is the key.

If you think about it, there is probably something big that is missing in your life. Maybe it is a friend you lost track of, an exercise program you used to do daily without fail, a talent you have not had time to nurture, or a promise to yourself that you broke years ago. Whatever it is, you feel the loss and it is important enough that you feel ready to make a commitment to bring it back.

This week you will create your own New Year's fairy tale and find this lost love in your life. You will take a trip down memory lane, identify something you'd like to enjoy once again, and take definite steps toward making that happen. Understand, though, that you can't fully bring back the past. Loved ones die. A broken relationship can't be "fixed" if someone has passed on, but you can find growth from his or her part in your life. People also change. You may find you no longer have much in common with your best friend from childhood, but you can enjoy shared experiences and use them to move on. Even places change. Pastures are converted into parking garages, and the tree you loved all those years ago might have been cut, or fallen down. Instead of trying to capture exactly what you had, catch the essence and re-commit to that.

Step 1: Identify Your Loss

Begin this week by taking some quiet time to think about all the great things in your past that once brought you joy. It might be a special pet you were fond of, or a fun activity that you did, or an extraordinary person who was part of your life. Of all the wonderful people, places and events you can think of, choose one to bring back into your life.

Some people need something more to motivate them than just a decision they made—some kind of commitment ceremony, or a formal statement among friends can give you more incentive to actually follow through. This week you could host a New Year's in July (or whatever month it is) party complete with paper hats and streamers. Have a big countdown at a certain hour, and after the countdown announce your re-commitment. It's a fun way to bring the support of your friends with you on your new adventure. Or, if you are doing *Success Within* as a group or with a partner, you might choose to have a picnic or a special dinner somewhere to commemorate your collective renewal commitments.

Step 2: Create the Time

Sometimes, before you bring whatever it is back to you, you need to reorganize certain areas of your life. It took me almost a year to clear enough time to spend a few hours a week at the barn. Enlist the aid of your family and juggle your schedule until it allows the time you need to pursue this new effort.

Step 3: Make the Effort

Now that you have allotted some time to actually make this a reality, detail the steps you need to take. If you loved making pottery in high school but haven't had the time (or money) to pursue it since, begin by finding all the options for making pottery in your area. A quick trip through the phone book, an Internet search, or a call to your local chamber of commerce can help you find what you need. Visit all your options, or at least talk with them on the phone. If money is an issue, volunteering or getting a part-time job at a pottery shop might be options. If clearing space so you have room for your clay, kiln, glazes and other equipment at home is more of an issue, put that on your "To Do" list. Maybe a corner of the basement or one side of the garage could be cleared and utilized. Keep going down your list of details, and before you know it, this activity will have once again become a regular part of your life.

Step 4: Merge Old and New
Remember that you can't fully bring back the past. Just as with my renewed commitment to horses, the way you bring your past into the present might be a little different. If there was a pet you loved and miss, it is possible that a pet in your home might now bother the allergies of another member of the household. So instead of having your own pet, think about volunteering at a local animal shelter or veterinarian's office. You could get a part time job grooming pets, or announce that you are willing to care for the pets of your friends while they are on vacation. Think positively and be creative. Where there is a will there is a way.

If you wish to renew a friendship, remember that the other person has to want this in their life as well. Sometimes it is enough for you to just tell them how much you treasured the time you spent together and that you have some wonderful memories that give you joy.

Week 31 Success Plan

* Identify something important that you've lost
* Make a commitment to bring it back into your life
* Create the time to make this happen
* Detail the steps and make the effort
* Be creative in merging the old with the new

Week 32

LET GO OF THE PAST

"Some think it's holding on that makes one strong; sometimes it's letting go." —Sylvia Robinson

In the early 1990s I had the privilege of working briefly with Lulu Roman. Lulu is the plus-sized singer, song-writer, and comedienne best known for her nearly twenty-five years on the hit television show *Hee Haw*. While Lulu has shared her gift of laughter with many, few know she was born with a thyroid dysfunction in a home for unwed mothers and placed in an orphanage. It was there that her weight became problematic and prevented her adoption. Her weight also made her the center of relentless teasing by the other children. As an emotional defense, Lulu found the power of humor, which later matured into a highly successful career as an actress and comedienne.

After spending a little time with Lulu I determined that there were two things about her that I found amazing. One was that she makes incredibly beautiful jewelry, and the other was that although she had endured a horrendous childhood—which led to an adult drug abuse problem—Lulu had finally been able to move on.

Lulu now uses her humor and her music to spread her personal message of hope to orphans everywhere through the Lulu Roman Orphans Project. It is her fondest hope that all orphans reach their full potential. Somewhere along the way, Lulu realized that she had the opportunity and the platform to turn her bad experience into a positive learning tool for others. She had learned to let go of her past and move on.

Experiences. We've all had thousands of them—both good and bad—and they make up much of who we are. Although it is nice to go back and revel in some of the great memories we've experienced in our lives, we need to let go of some of the other, more negative, memories. Over the years I have known several people who just love to wallow in the negative recesses of their past. You probably know someone like this, too. She might sit around moaning and complaining about how unfair life is and lament about all her "if onlys." Her negativity makes her hard to be around. She is using a bad event that happened to her—or several bad events—as an excuse for not accomplishing the many great things she is still capable of doing. No one lives a perfect childhood or has a perfect marriage. Fairy tales are fiction. But everyone can learn to take a negative circumstance they've been given, use it, move past it, and have a full life.

I once heard a motivational speaker on the radio who had lost both legs and an arm in a tragic car accident. During the interview, he said something that I will remember forever. He said that he no longer focuses on the nine thousand things that he can no longer do, but on the one thousand things that he still *can* do. Whenever I feel down I remember that man, whose name I never learned.

Razzy Bailey is a man whose name is far more familiar to me because for several years I managed his career. During Razzy's more than thirty-year marriage to his first wife, Sandra, she developed emotional problems and eventually took her own life. I'll never forget the numbness in Razzy's voice when he called to tell me what had happened, and I soon realized how devastated Razzy was. Yet just a few days later, Razzy asked if I could set up an interview with WSM-AM, a radio station that at the time covered areas of thirty-eight states and was broadcast around the world via satellite. Instead of choosing to be haunted by Sandra's death, Razzy chose to talk about it in hopes that his words would prevent the same tragedy from happening to another family. And it did. We received several letters from people who said Razzy's interview helped save them or a family member.

I was so proud of Razzy during that time. He could have chosen to cancel tour dates, to put his career on hold, and no one would have thought less of him. Instead, he wanted people to hear the raw emotion in his voice, to understand how terrible suicide was for the survivors. He realized that nothing he or anyone else could do would bring Sandra back, but he could a) help others and b) move on and live the rest of his life fully, which he has.

Hopefully you have not had to deal with suicide or a dysfunctional childhood, but even if you have, you are not alone. Sooner or later something happens to just about everyone. You can't change the event, but you can choose to learn from the experience and, like Lulu and Razzy, you can learn to help others while you move on.

Step 1: Get it All Out
Okay. This is your one and only chance to get it all out, to dredge up all the awfulness in your life. Take an hour, or an evening, to grieve. Allow yourself, for a few minutes, to let the emotion out, to feel all the pain and anger and resent-

ment that your bad experiences have brought. If it helps, bring a friend along on this little journey, or do it in the safety of a small support group. Others may prefer to walk this particular path alone. If you've had a lot of negatives in your life, you may choose instead to pick one event rather than deal with all of them at once.

Step 2: Get Over it

Time is up. Get over it and move on. I know that's easier said than done, but here are a few tips that might move you along a little faster. Let's say at some point in your life that you were raped. Rape is a terrible, tragic, life-shattering event, but rather than dwell on all the negative aspects, choose instead to know that you are now uniquely qualified to counsel others who have had the same experience. You could talk to high school students and give them prevention tips or a list of things to do if it happens to them. You could train and volunteer as a rape crisis counselor. You could use the experience as personal motivation to earn a black belt in karate or to teach others about personal defense. Rather than focus on what the rape took from you, focus on what the experience can give you.

If you have lost someone in your life tragically, take time to mourn, but then celebrate and honor his life. If it was a traffic accident, ask if you could say a few words to reckless drivers at the next local traffic school, or you could talk to kids who are taking driver's ed classes. Better yet, become a part-time driving instructor, or become a public speaker and talk to local groups about the importance of safe driving. If you lost a child who loved art, start a scholarship in his name. You could ask local artists to donate a work of art and hold an annual silent auction with the proceeds going to the scholarship fund. There are tons of possibilities if you just focus on the positive rather than the negative.

Step 3: Get Specific

Find some special gift that you have been given as a result of sadness or tragedy. Thousands of other people found theirs; you can find something, too. Now develop a specific way you can use that gift to help others. Research the idea by talking with groups or individuals who could benefit from your experience, then detail the steps you need to take to make it happen. Only by helping someone else can you truly let go. In the process, you will meet some wonderful people and create many new and positive moments to share and remember fondly.

Week 32 Success Plan

* Let yourself grieve
* Move on by finding something positive or gained in the experience
* Develop a specific plan to help or prevent
* Work the plan and enjoy many great new experiences

Week 33

COUNT YOUR BLESSINGS

"When I started counting my blessings, my whole life turned around." —Willie Nelson

Despite the intensive, never-ending marketing that happens in today's world, we really only need a few comforts to be happy. Once food, clothing, transportation and shelter are covered, everything else is really icing on the cake. Of course, we all want more, and there is nothing wrong with that as long as you can pay for it and understand that you really don't need it.

We did not have a lot of money when I was growing up. Yet I still managed to have a horse and compete in local horse shows. My mother helped some, but by the time I was fourteen, I also raked yards, babysat, and gave both flute and riding lessons to earn money.

Back then I didn't arrive at the shows in a truck and horse trailer like the other competitors. Instead, I had a little governess cart. You've probably seen them in movies, especially British movies made in the forties and fifties. The cart is a big wicker basket and the driver sits sideways on a bench. In the movies, the cart is often filled with cheery, apple-cheeked cherubs and they are singing a song in three-part harmony. My cart was made of wood and had truck tires instead of the large elegantly spoked wooden wheels seen on film. And instead of chubby children, my cart was filled with the tack, clothes, and grooming supplies I'd need for the day. As it is difficult to sing three-part harmony by yourself (although I did hear singer/songwriter David Allan

Coe do it once) my horse, Snoqualmie, and I listened to the early morning polka review on a battery-operated AM radio.

It never bothered me that I tied my horse to a tree rather than to a horse trailer, or that my saddle cost fifty-dollars, while the saddle of the rider next to me cost five hundred. I just made do with what I had and worked twice as hard. In hindsight, it was a great situation for me. It gave me a wonderful work ethic, which I maintain to this day. I took better care of my equipment than the other riders did because I knew if anything became damaged, it would be difficult to replace. It also made me shop smarter for my brushes, clothes and equipment, and I quickly learned to determine the best value for the price.

Many mornings at the edge of a certain cornfield, a red fox would follow my cart. I looked forward to seeing him, and would never have known he existed if I'd traveled by truck and trailer. I was able to observe the show grounds as I slowly approached. I could savor the anticipation and scope out who was parked where. By the time I arrived, I knew just where to pull in and tie up. In short, I greatly enjoyed the little extras that my situation brought me, and know I would have missed out on a lot had I had the money to travel to the shows in the conventional manner.

While I was writing this book, a man named Fred Hale Sr. died in his sleep. At the time of his death, he was twelve days away from his one hundred and fourteenth birthday and had been documented as the world's oldest man. According to his obituary, he had retired some fifty years prior to his death from careers as a railroad postal worker and beekeeper, and enjoyed gardening, canning fruits and vegetables, and making homemade applesauce. At age ninety-five, Mr. Hale flew to Japan to visit a grandson who was in the Navy. While en route back to the United States, he stopped in Hawaii to give boogie-boarding a try. At one hundred three years of age, Hale still lived on his own, and was able to shovel snow from his rooftop. Hale also was a Guinness record-holder for the oldest driver. At age one hundred eight, he said he still found slow drivers annoying.

I never had the opportunity to meet Fred Hale Sr., but it sounds as if he led a full and interesting life. What I found most fascinating, though, was the fact that his obituary also stated that Fred Hale Sr. didn't need a lot to be happy. He had apparently found love, happiness and fulfillment without the benefit of fame or fortune, without the fancy car or the castle in the hills. This man had learned to find enjoyment in the little things in life and was happy with what he had.

This week you too will discover there is much around you to enjoy and to be thankful for, for life's little pleasures are certainly our greatest.

Step 1: Recognize the Blessings in Your Life

There are blessings all around us that we are not even aware of. The first step this week is to recognize the efforts of others in our lives. Think about all the people around you who help make your day a little easier. When was the last time you thanked your partner or spouse for their financial contributions to the household—or their daily attention to details that make your life run more smoothly? What about the cleaning crew who cleans your office, or your grandchildren's scout leaders? After a few minutes of thought, you may be quite surprised with all the people who contribute in many different ways to your life. So take a few minutes to mentally recognize everyone in your life whose efforts help you each and every day.

Step 2: Acknowledge Those Who Make it Happen

Once you have identified the little blessings in your life, acknowledge the people who made it happen. You could write a thank you card, or treat a special friend to dinner. Or, if possible, you could just thank him or her verbally. Whatever the method, these people will know they are appreciated.

Step 3: Find Things That You Appreciate

Now think about all the items in your life—everything from your car or dishwasher, to your television, CDs, DVDs and radio—and understand that many people do not have these things. Sure, maybe the water pressure in your apartment is a little low, but there are many people who have no place to live at all. And, there are others who don't have any water. Yes, you should try to do something to bring the water pressure back up, but in the meantime, know that it would be much worse if you had no apartment or water. Make a list of all these wonders in your life and as the list grows, you will realize that you are truly blessed.

Step 4: Choose Your Biggest Blessing of the Day

At the end of every day this week, take the time to acknowledge your biggest blessing of the day. Maybe it was the sunny smile on your child's face. Or it could have been the car repair that was a hundred dollars less than quoted.

Maybe it was the simple unexpected sight of a robin or a rainbow, or a kid skipping on the street that made you smile and turned your day totally around. If you look, you will find these moments all around you. Some will even be big enough to hang on to and cherish for days to come.

Week 33 Success Plan

* Recognize the many people who are blessings in your life
* Thank those who made it possible
* Make a list of the things you are privileged to have
* Identify your biggest blessing every day

HONESTY IS THE BEST POLICY

"Honesty is the best policy. If I lose mine honor, I lose myself."
—William Shakespeare

When I was just two years old, I stole a small plastic horse from my nursery school. I remember the event clearly. The horse was part of a small barnyard set and was a rich brown with a large black patch on top of his rump. Even then I knew horses didn't have patches like that in real life, but I wanted that horse so badly I couldn't stand it. One day when I was wearing a pair of blue overalls I just slipped the horse into my pocket and took him home, where he became an immediate source of conflicted joy.

I played with him often as a child, but I always felt guilty that I had taken him away from his barnyard friends. Even then I knew it was the wrong thing to do. When I was thirty it was way too late to confess to my nursery school teacher, but I finally told my mother what I had done. Even though my confession was long past due, it felt really good to have it out in the open. The best part of the entire incident is that I never stole another thing in my life. Early on I learned that honesty is the best policy.

It can be very difficult to be honest, both with yourself and with others. Life deals us very strange hands sometimes and it can be tough to know quite the right thing to do. It is also difficult—if not impossible—for people to see themselves as others do. Seeing yourself from another perspective can be helpful if you are interested in improving specific areas of your life. You may not even realize that you are perceived as being overbearing, or sweet, or tough, or fair. But, if you understand how others see you, you can better understand your weak areas and be more effective in overcoming them.

Seeing yourself from an outside perspective takes a little strength, because you may not always like what you see. But you will also discover what motivates you, where your principles are, and what you will or will not do. With my little plastic horse, I learned that wanting something so badly that you do something wrong to get it is not worth it—the guilt feelings can overwhelm you!

A series of questions kicks off this week's exercises. And when you're done pondering the answers, you may well find that your view of yourself has changed dramatically. Follow it up with some honest feedback from those around you and you may end up an entirely new person.

Step 1: How Far Will You Go?

1. We often do not know how honest we really are until we get into a situation that tests us. Here are some questions about honesty that have no right or wrong answers. Take time to think about them and what you would do if you were actually in this situation. For fun, you might discuss these questions with your family around the dinner table, or with a group of friends.

2. If one hundred people were chosen randomly, how many of them do you think would be more honest than you are?

3. Would you lie if it helped a friend? Would you lie if it helped a friend but hurt someone else?

4. If you saw money lying in plain sight on a desk or table would you take it? How much or little would the amount have to be for you to consider taking it? Would you be more likely to take it from a friend, or a stranger?

5. If you found one thousand dollars lying in a parking lot, would you take it, or would you turn it in to the police?

6. Pretend you are taking a test. It could be a driver's exam, a civil service test, or a test for school. If you knew without a doubt that if you cheated on this test that you would not be caught, would you cheat?

7. If someone offered you a large sum of cash in exchange for confidential information about the company you work for or the church you attend, would you take it? If so, how large would the sum have to be?

8. If you purchased something at a store and they did not charge you enough for it, would you point out the error?

9. Do you ever exaggerate? If so, when and why?

10. If you knew a close friend or relative had lied to you, how would you handle the situation?

11. Can you be trusted to do what you say you are going to do? Why or why not?

12. If you were given a million dollars on the condition that you had to give it all away, to whom would you give it and why?

Step 2: Ask Others for Honest Opinions

Now let's take it a step further. Based on the answers to your questions in Step 1, ask for feedback from a few people. For example, whenever I pitch a new client to the media, I am very interested in the reaction we get. If everyone has similar comments, such as the client doesn't give enough information, or they need to update their image, I take it seriously and we do our best to fix the problem. If the comments are very different from one another (i.e. one says the client talks too much, another doesn't like the client's message, a third thinks a better haircut would help attract national television) it's usually just personal opinion and does not indicate any major problem areas. You, for example, might ask a few people you know if they consider you trustworthy.

Do people think you exaggerate?
Do people feel they can trust you to hold confidences?
Do people consider you basically honest?
Do people think it is sometimes hard for you to do the right thing?
Would people trust you with their kids, with their money, to water their plants when they were away?

You might get the same sort of answer from everyone, or all kinds of different answers. It's the answers that are all the same that you should take an honest look at. Maybe everyone said they trusted you not to take money, but they didn't trust you to follow through. Whatever the feedback, if a strong majority say similar things, take a step back and consider what they are saying, especially if the answers from those around you contrasted sharply with your own answers.

You may also be pleasantly surprised at the feedback you receive. You could find out how well-liked you are, or discover positive qualities you didn't even know you had.

Step 3: Honestly Evaluate

Lastly this week, take the information you received from others in Step 2 and evaluate it. If their answers about you were consistently different from your perception of yourself, think hard about why others see you so differently than you see yourself. Think about why people trust you in certain areas but not in others. Are you worthy of trust? Do you feel you are not quite as honest as you'd like to be? What can you do to change that? What areas of honesty, integrity and trust are hard for you? Use the information as a positive tool to improve yourself.

Week 34 Success Plan

* Think about and answer the questions about honesty
* Based on your answers choose a few areas about yourself to ask others
* Use their answers to better identify and strengthen weak areas

Week 35

THE GENERATION GAP

"It is my firm belief that I have a link with the past and a responsibility to the future. I cannot give up. I cannot despair. There's a whole future, generations to come. I have to keep trying."
—King Hussein

My son had a lot of trouble being a young teenager. So much so that he was twice sent to group homes. At the second home he became friends with a middle-aged former drug dealer. This may seem at first glance like an unlikely—and unsafe—friendship. But once Colby was able to discover the extreme hardships the older man had endured, and why he made the life choices he had, he learned to respect his new friend. My son learned a lot about life from his older friend. And, I think his friend received satisfaction from passing his life mistakes along to a member of the younger generation, with hope that the mistakes would not be repeated.

It is important to realize that everyone, no matter which generation they are from, has something of value to teach. The world is a constantly changing place and the younger generation can help those more advanced in years in some areas, and the older generation can help the younger in others.

I first realized that concept when Colby was three. We somehow got into a silly argument about the color of the outside of the Crystal fast-food restaurants. I insisted they were orange, he maintained they were red. I thought he was unaware of the difference in colors. He was adamant that he was right . . . and he was. Imagine how foolish I felt, arguing the wrong side with a three-year-old. But I never again assumed that just because he was a child that he was wrong and I was right. Over the years he, and other children, have taught me many other lessons. Although children might be young in years, they have knowledge to share.

And what of the older generation? Their experience, knowledge and wisdom should count for much. Even though technology has passed many by, the efforts of those who came before us are what got us to where we are now. Older generations also have fascinating stories to tell about their lives and the lives of those who came before them. We all should listen far more than we do.

One of the biggest concerns in relationships between the generations is finding common interests. What can a twenty-year-old person possibly have in common with a person who is sixty, or seventy? You might be surprised. I recently edited a manuscript about the legendary film star Cary Grant. A man named Bill Royce, who was one of Cary's best friends, wrote it. At the time they met, Bill was twenty-five and Cary was just shy of his seventieth birthday. At first glance, you might wonder what on earth they had in common. It turns out a lot. Both did not know much about their birth mothers, both had abusive and disadvantaged childhoods, both shared a love of music and an interest in psychology. Bill helped Cary learn about the newer popular musical artists of the day, while Cary helped Bill deal with the tragedies of his past. Together the two enjoyed movies, great conversation, and many unforgettable outings. It was a very strong friendship and lasted until Cary's death some twelve years later. The difference in ages was not a problem. In fact, it enhanced the relationship, as each was able to learn something from the other. Sometimes difference in age can be a wonderful experience.

One of the best situations I could ever have stumbled across as a young publicist was to have worked very early in my career with some of the outlaw legends of the music industry, including, among others, David Allan Coe, Johnny PayCheck, Razzy Bailey, and TomPall Glaser. I learned more from them than I could have learned if I had gotten a doctoral degree in public relations. They were full of stories of events that helped shape the music industry into what it is today, because they had not only lived that history, they had created it. Between them they had already experienced every public relations success and downfall possible, and their names opened huge doors with the media. Thank goodness I recognized the many opportunities these people gave me, and I picked their brains every chance I had. Since then, I am thankful to have had opportunities to pass that knowledge along to others in the entertainment industry.

It is a lot of fun having friends from different generations. It opens many doors that would otherwise remain closed. This week, you will challenge yourself more than once as you too become closer to someone of a different generation.

Step 1: Target a Generation
If you either have many years under your belt, or if you have just a few, it will be an easy choice for you to target either an older generation or one that is younger. Those who

are in the middle will have a more difficult time, because they have the opportunity to choose either direction.

So where do you find people who are considerably older or younger? Everywhere. If you have a person in your family such as a grandparent, a great-aunt or -uncle, or a great-grandchild, family gatherings and holidays might provide a perfect opportunity to get to know that individual better. You may also have a special interest in a specific generation, and that opens the door for you to volunteer at preschools, nursing homes, senior centers or children's camps. Maybe you already volunteer somewhere where people of a variety of ages help out. At least one of them is bound to be fascinating. You could coach an over-fifty baseball team or a team of four-year-old soccer players, or you could become a big brother or sister, or adopt a grandparent.

You could do this as a family project, by yourself, or with a partner or a church or a social group. You could even befriend an older or younger person at the office or the gym or at church. Other options include providing special enrichment classes for seniors once a week, once a month, or once a year. You could even become a special friend to an elementary school class. Taking a senior to the grocery store every now and then is also a great way to get to know a new friend.

Your individual time constraints and interests are unique to you. Use them to get to know someone older or younger. The choices are many and they are all yours.

Step 2: Find Common Ground
and Embrace the Differences
Once you have found someone (or a group of someones) to

get to know better, decide how, specifically, you will learn from them. If this person is a distant relative a continent away you might have to converse via phone, email or letters. If your best friend's grandchild visits often, you could participate in some of their activities.

But just how do you begin to talk with a person you don't even know? Relax and be yourself. Talk neither up nor down, no matter what age he or she might be; just talk as if you were talking with a very good friend. You can begin with casual conversation. Pay a sincere compliment, or ask questions about the little things in his or her life: work, homework, family, or other activities this individual finds fun. Keep it casual and remember that this other person has to want to reach out, too. If he is a co-worker, ask about his background, or if he has any ideas on a different way to complete a task. If you take the friendship slowly and do not judge, it won't be too long before you are finding many common threads in your lives.

If you have found a group of people of different generations, your one-on-one experiences will be fewer, but you may learn more about the other generation as a whole. We've all had different experiences based on the general time frame in which we were born. Some of us remember President Kennedy getting shot, others don't. You will gain a lot of insight from sharing your own experiences as you learn about those of another time. Know that every person is capable of changing your life with just a few words. Use every opportunity you can to ask about other people's thoughts and feelings. You may not agree, but you may begin to understand.

Step 3: Enjoy Shared Experiences

Shared experiences can bring the most unlikely people together, even those of different generations. You could ask an older friend to participate in an oral history, or a younger friend to help you put together a scrapbook as a gift for a mutual friend. Your shared experience could be a quick trip to the doctor with an elderly friend. That would provide a great opportunity to inquire how the experience has changed over her lifetime. How have doctors, doctor's appointments and medical science changed over the years? When your elderly friend was a child, the doctor may have even come to her home by horse and buggy. A lot of fun and laughter is sure to occur as we cross the generation gap.

Week 35 Success Plan

* Choose a generation
* Find common ground
* Embrace the differences
* Share a project

Week 36

LEARN SOMETHING NEW EVERY DAY

"To know wisdom and instruction; to perceive the words of under-standing." —Proverbs 1:2

Have you learned anything new today? Did you learn that you really like wearing red hats, or that your partner has a new interest in tennis? Did you learn to fix a leaky faucet or realize that cornstarch can be used to treat heat rashes? How about fish? Did you know they can get seasick if swirled in a pail or kept on board a rolling ship? I love getting up in the morning because I know every day will bring some new and unexpected piece of knowledge.

Some of the information you might learn is silly, trivial or fun. You never know when trotting out a piece of information such as the fact that Groundhog Day originated in 16th century Germany might come in handy. And, letting your friends know that a British merchant named Peter Durand developed the can opener in 1810 can be impressive. Here are a few other fun tidbits you can throw out:

Pancakes were cooked in ancient Egypt
Francis Bellamy of Rome, New York wrote the "Pledge of Allegiance" in 1892
Catnip is a member of the mint family
A horse has no collarbone
The name Carol is traditionally a feminine form of Charles

But not all information or learning is trivial. Today you might unexpectedly stumble across information that could help you in your work—the discovery of a new processing method, or viewing a news segment that can help you help a client. Or, today might be the day you learn your child is a nature enthusiast, or is excelling in reading. You never know what the day will bring, and half the fun is in the surprises.

Your day might also bring prospects for learning in areas other than information. Maybe you have a chance to check out a new restaurant and a new dish. From this you could learn that you like the restaurant, and you (still) don't like anchovies. Or you could watch a television program you have not seen before, or walk down an unfamiliar street. These activities all offer chances to learn something: on your walk you discover you like the unique shape of the mailbox in front of number 417, but don't care for the landscaping at 415.

How will you use that information? Who knows? But throughout each day learning comes in all sorts of shapes and forms. It is up to you to decide which of the many opportunities you will take.

Years ago when our neighbors moved out of our shared duplex, they left behind an old, rickety child's bicycle. My son was only four years old at the time and the bike was much too large for him, but Colby was bound and determined to learn to ride it. I thought, at worst, that it was an activity that would keep him occupied for a few hours, but after spending two days getting on and falling off, and getting on and falling off, Colby learned to ride that bike. In the abandoned bicycle, Colby recognized an opportunity to learn something new—and grabbed it.

As you begin to recognize all the different ways to learn, you will find yourself automatically choosing activities in which you know you will learn something. And as you learn more and more, you will find yourself looking forward to each new day with a sense of anticipation likely unmatched since childhood. You might also find yourself developing some brand new interests in life. Congratulations, you have just rediscovered the love of learning.

Malcolm Forbes was a man who understood this process. Before his death, he was one of the wealthiest men in the country, yet he continually made comments about the importance of knowledge, saying, "The dumbest people I know are those who know it all," "Education's purpose is to replace an empty mind with an open one," and "It's so much easier to suggest solutions when you don't know too much about the problem." Malcolm Forbes knew that every day gave him the chance to learn something new that could help him, his family, or his business. Even better, every day you, too, can pass on what you have learned to someone else.

This week you will surprise both yourself and others as you acknowledge all that you learn every day.

Step 1: Make a Daily Learning List

Recognize that this week begins a brand new chapter in your life. When you wake up every day from now on, you will know that everyone you meet, every situation you find yourself in, and every minute of every hour of the day will teach you something. Grab a sheet of paper (or two) and carry it with you this entire week. Every time you learn something new jot it down. It doesn't matter if what you learn is trivial or fun, important or just plain weird. Add all the things you discover to your list. You might be surprised at how much you learn each day; if you are like most people, your list could get quite long! You may not yet know how you are going to apply all your new pieces of knowledge, but someday you will know exactly what to do with them.

Step 2: Big Learn of the Day

At the end of each day, choose the one thing you learned that is most important, or is most applicable in your life. As you go through your list, create an additional list featuring these "big learns" of the day. At the end of the week you will probably see a trend. You may have chosen a group of experiences relating to work, relationships, or lessons of practical use. It is helpful to know what areas you have chosen for your big learn of the day, as it is a strong indicator of where your interests or concerns are at this time of your life. Take time at the end of the week to see if you can spot any trends and discover what, if anything, it might mean. There are no right or wrong answers here, but it is helpful information to know about yourself. If you do this again in several months, it is quite likely that your big learns of the day will be in a totally different area, indicating new areas that are now of more importance to you.

Step 3: Pass it On

Every day, be sure to pass along at least one new thing that you learned. Or have a contest with a friend to see how many new ideas you can pass along to others. This is always fun because you never know what circumstances will arise that will give you the opportunity to pass information along. Be sure to credit the source of your new information by saying something like, "Billy is so smart. He let me know that . . ." You will make whomever gave you the information feel wonderful, and it will encourage them in their own efforts to learn.

Week 36 Success Plan

* Make a daily learning list and write down all you have learned
* Choose one item to be your big learn of the day
* Recognize the trends in your big learns and discover what they mean
* Every day pass on at least one new thing you learned
* Credit the source of your newfound knowledge

Week 37

ALL OR NOTHING

"Life is either a great adventure or nothing."
—Helen Keller

I am always struck by the saga of Christopher Reeve, the well-known actor who became paralyzed after a fall from a horse. After the accident, Chris devoted every waking moment to regaining control over his body. Day after day, year after year, he worked on his goal. And while he did not reach his target of walking before he died, he did make incredible strides. He could move some of his fingers—a feat his many doctors swore was physically impossible. He regained feeling over much of his body—another milestone the medical community said was not possible. He could even breathe some of the time on his own, yet another impossibility, according to modern medicine. Chris accomplished these miracles solely because of the great effort he put into his goal.

Often when we do not reach our goals it's because there isn't enough concentrated energy put behind the idea or the relationship; there is not enough focus placed directly on the goal. How many times have you tried to do something and did not accomplish it? If you are like me, probably hundreds of times. Maybe your goal was to lose ten pounds—or twenty—and it never happened. Your goal could have been cleaning out the garage, becoming closer to your daughter, learning to bake pies, becoming less sensitive, or any number of things. Or, it could be a whole series of nothings, because they never happened.

I have a closet in my bathroom that I have been meaning to organize since I moved into my house over seven years ago. Surely in seven years I could have found a spare hour to organize a closet. It hasn't happened simply because I haven't wanted it badly enough. Unlike my earlier success in business and in the show ring, there are many goals I want to reach far more than having an organized bathroom closet. Someday it will get moved up my list of priorities, but not today.

When was the last time you gave something your all, when you devoted every spare ounce of time and energy to the one thing that you are most passionate about, the one person, place or event that is most important in your life at this particular moment? Sadly, so many of us are so busy multitasking that we do not have the focus to put toward just one area; we are too busy doing three activities at once.

This week that will change. This week you will target one thing that is very, very important to you and you will work as if your life depended on its success. You will make it a priority and devote every single spare moment you can to the success of your project.

Let's say you want to lower your blood pressure. Your doctor has cautioned that it is creeping ever higher and you need to take action now, before it gets out of hand. But taking action means making sacrifices. It means it's going to be hard to do. It means you have to think about it and plan around it, and give up doughnuts and chocolate chip cookies and (gasp!) start to exercise. You will have to research the condition and decide the best plan of attack. In short, it's going to be a whole lot of work.

Consider, then, the alternative. Eventual heart attack? Stroke? Either could be disabling, or even fatal. Your half-hearted attempts to lower the count have landed you no-where thus far, but this week you will change that. To make a change, however, you have to find motivation. You have to want to lower your blood pressure so badly you can taste it. You have to want it more than you've wanted anything in recent history.

If the thought of a heart attack or stroke is not motiva-tion enough, (and it probably isn't because none of that stuff will ever really happen to you, will it?) then maybe your mo-tivation is your family. What would they do without you around? Is it fair to ask them to care for you long-term, years before you or they are mentally or financially prepared to do so? It could be your loss of independence, or maybe you hate hospitals. Or maybe your motivation is being able to have a doughnut as a reward once you have achieved a certain milestone. Or, when you've reached your target count, you could reward yourself with a trip to some exotic place (or a weekend getaway to the Holiday Inn). Only you know what your motivation is and where you will find it.

My friend Carol Grace Anderson overcame all odds to become an in-demand, nationally recognized public speaker only because she was incredibly motivated. Carol and her three siblings were raised in a tiny eighteen-foot travel trailer with two wheels, no bathroom and no air conditioning. The trailer was parked in New Jersey very close to many other trailers, and most of her neighbors were circus performers. In high school, Carol was told time and time again that she was not college material, yet she persevered and was ac-cepted at three different colleges—and flunked out three times. She readjusted her plan of attack and started back at a junior college one class at a time. Eventually she earned a Masters degree in Counselor Education. And later, she sang with the Roy Clark Show, toured around the world, landed a speaking role in a major motion picture, wrote four books, and performed on *The Tonight Show*.

What was Carol's motivation? She didn't want to live in an eighteen-foot trailer the rest of her life and she knew she needed an education before she could make her own way in the world. Her plan was very simple: remain focused, pour all energy into the goal, and stay with it until the task is completed.

The success plan for this week involves giving one thing everything you've got. Just think how good you will feel once you have lowered your blood pressure, or quit smoking, painted the porch, or called a truce to the feud with your grandfather. You will have the great satisfaction of having accomplished something that is important to you, and it really is very easy to do. It's all about motivation and focus. Whatever your goal, stand back and watch the results pour in.

Step 1: Choose Your Goal

First decide what it is that you will devote your time and energies to. I once knew a lady whose greatest wish in life was to own a video copy of every John Wayne movie in existence. She eventually collected all but two (he made well over one-hundred movies) and was interviewed on local radio and television numerous times throughout her quest. The interviews even brought her leads on some of the harder-to-find films.

There is certain to be something in your life that is important to you that you have not yet accomplished. It can be a little thing or a big thing, serious or fun. The only criterion is that you must really, *really* want to get this done.

Step 2: Find Your Motivation

Once you decide what it is that you are going to do, find your motivation. Find your reason. When the going gets tough (or you have difficulty allotting time) you will need something to draw from. You will need to have something that will carry you along even when you want to throw in the towel and forget it all. There must be something that will give you the motivation to succeed. Find it.

Step 3: Make a Plan

Now make a plan—a realistic plan. How long will this project take you and where will you find the time? How will you accomplish your plan? Will you need help from friends or family? Are there monetary costs involved and if so, where will the money come from? Decide in detail exactly how you will take this goal from thought to reality.

Step 4: Stay the Course

Once you begin you may have periods of doubt, times when you find it much easier to sit on the couch and watch another *Andy Griffith* rerun instead of working on your goal. Go back to your motivation and dig deeper. Keep the end result in mind. You know you can do this!

Week 37 Success Plan

* Choose your goal
* Find a reason that will keep you motivated
* Develop a realistic plan
* Stay on it until it's done

BE AN EXPERT

*"Try, try, try, and keep on trying is the rule that must be followed
to become an expert in anything."*
—W. Clement Stone

Everyone should be able to do something really well, or
be an expert in at least one subject. Some people excel
during emergencies; others are really good at passing along
a smile. Another's gift could be fixing cars, or playing tennis, or caring for pets. Everyone should excel at something.
It gives you a tremendous amount of self-esteem and allows
you to pass some of your expert knowledge or skill to others.

Kay Johnson, one of the presidents of the International
Fan Club Organization, bakes what are probably the best
cookies on Earth. She also receives personal joy by giving
her cookies to others. Kay has many other talents, but she is
definitely an expert cookie baker, and everyone needs great
cookies once in awhile.

Kay's expertise is in doing, but some people's expertise
is more of an extension of themselves. My friend Lee Allen
is one of the most knowledgeable people around on the history of books, but she is also an expert listener. She is the
kind of person who—just minutes after meeting her—people
want to pour out their heartaches and troubles. She has a
real gift and has helped hundreds of people through hard
times just by lending—for a few short minutes—an ear.

Other people, like my former client Paul Overstreet, have expertise in creating. Paul is the music industry's go-to guy for lyrics that help keep marriages and families together. Paul's parents divorced when he was very young, and fairly early in his life Paul decided he wanted to help prevent that from happening to other families. He does it through his music and his songs. Those in the music industry know if they want a song that lyrically promotes home and family in a touching—or humorous—way, Paul is the man. At this one particular skill, there is no one better.

Where is your expertise? Are you a doer like Kay, or someone like Lee whose expertise is an extension of her personality, or are you a creator like Paul? If you already have found a subject or skill in which you are an expert, this is your chance to learn even more about your chosen field.

Learning opportunities are all around you no matter what your current level, and most of them cost very little, if anything at all. If you have cable or satellite television, there are shows on a variety of cable stations that cover many different subjects. In thumbing through my cable guide, today alone I had the choice of watching the rise and fall of Adolph Hitler, comparisons of antique mirrors, cooking nutritional snacks for pets, the history of the Corvette, or medical breakthroughs for hyperactivity—and that was all in the same hour.

The Internet also offers a plethora of learning possibilities. There are virtually hundreds of sites on every possible subject, and they present widely varying thoughts, ideas, and opinions. There are libraries, bookstores, magazines, mentors, coaches, teachers, support groups and special interest groups. No matter how much or how little you know about your chosen subject of expertise, there is always more to learn—and someone or some way to help you.

If you haven't yet found your expertise, this week will help point you in the right direction. Make a list of interests that you are good at and passionate about. When I was in high school, I played the flute. I practiced several hours each day and could hold my own with other top high school flautists around the country. Although talented, I did not have nearly as much passion for the flute as I did for horses. You must have passion in order to invest the time and effort to become an expert.

Your area of expertise could be virtually anything. It could be collecting something, or the study of a certain area of history. Here in Nashville we have a number of people who are experts on the Civil War, or on specific battles of the Civil War. You could be like songwriter Chalee Tennison and be an expert with a glue gun. Chalee knows more about arts and crafts than anyone I've ever met. If you can glue it together and make something out of it, Chalee knows how to do it.

Depending on what you do for a living, you could become an expert in your field, or a certain area of your field. Study and learn all you can. Your knowledge will raise your value in your industry and might lead to new ideas or breakthroughs.

As your interest, knowledge, skill, and expertise grow, you will likely come into contact with others of similar interests, which in turn expands your circle of friends and acquaintances. Some of life's greatest moments emerge when we are living our passion. Be sure to take time this week to hone your expertise and enjoy the rewards that follow.

Step 1: What is Your Expertise?

First, identify your specific expertise, or the area in which you hope to someday become an expert. This will either be a ridiculously easy task for you, or one that could take much thought. You may already be an expert in a particular area and choose a second, or third topic to study. Go for it! Let your imagination fly; once you make the decision to learn, you can learn about anything—and everything—that interests you.

Or, you may choose to learn about a different area of your current expertise. If you have a passion for playing the guitar or piano, you could learn about the history of the instrument or research new breakthroughs. You could find information on your instrument's impact on society or become an expert on interesting stories relating to your instrument. Or, study how the piano or guitar is used creatively in different parts of the world, or learn about interesting people who have played the instrument.

Step 2: Learn More

Make active strides in learning more. My son has a learning disability called dysgraphia, which is difficulty in the mechanics of writing. He has a brilliant mind and reads exceedingly well, but any kind of writing is frustrating for him and significantly slows down his learning process. I home schooled Colby for many years and am very aware of the fact that every person learns a little bit differently. For those who do not learn easily in the traditional method, mention of anything that sounds as if it involves exhaustive reading and tedious note-taking can be intimidating. So if reading and notes and adult extension classes are not your bag, know that you can learn a lot by watching an informative DVD or a television show. You could listen to a radio program, go to a museum or a seminar, or visit an expert who is involved in whatever it is you want to learn. Be creative; open your mind.

Step 3: Give Back

There is nothing more rewarding than passing along your knowledge. And, as an expert, you have a duty to spread the fruits of your labors. As you learn and grow in your specific area, begin thinking of ways that you could teach other people. Depending on your subject, Boy and Girl Scout groups are always looking for people to come in and give a short presentation. Those organizations have badges for just about everything. Also 4-H, FFA, Junior Leader, and a host of other youth groups would be happy for you to share your knowledge, as would many elementary or middle school teachers. Be sure to remember to think about seniors, civic, and church groups, too. Who knows, maybe you will open a new career path for a boy who is currently floundering, or introduce a bored girl to a new and rewarding life-long hobby or interest. What an incredible gift that would be to you both.

Week 38 Success Plan

* Define your subject matter
* Be creative in learning all you can
* Find ways to share your knowledge

Week 39

REPEAT, REPEAT, REPEAT

"It's the repetition of affirmations that leads to belief. And once that belief becomes a deep conviction, things begin to happen."
—Muhammad Ali

Well, we're at the end of Part 3 and it is time for a quick review. As always, it is your choice whether to go back and revisit certain parts of the past twelve weeks or to move on to Part 4. The following questions might help you make that decision:

Since you began *Success Within*, what great things have happened in your life?

Have you met any new friends?

Have you learned anything new?

Have you been able to teach anyone anything?

How do you feel about yourself now, compared to before you began *Success Within*?

How have your priorities changed?

Do you look at any group or groups of people differently?

Have you incorporated any new activities into your life?

How have your relationships with those closest to you changed?

You should have some pretty specific answers to those questions. If you don't, you might need to go back and revisit some of the weeks' activities. *Success Within* is a lot like going to college. You get out of it exactly what you put in.

Just being there doesn't always cut it—you have to actually participate to get the most out of the experience. Then, if you don't get it the first time, you need to go over it again and again until you derive benefits.

I know a few people, and you probably do too, who seem to make the same mistakes in life over and over again. For some reason, they are repeating the process time after time until they either get it right or something positive happens. The trick is to keep the mistakes from becoming habit, and to keep learning something from the repetitive experiences.

Billy Ray Cyrus, most recently the star of the PAX television series *Doc*, knows all about repetitive experiences. For something like five years he drove from his home in the Ashland, Kentucky area to Nashville, knocking on doors every Monday week after week, month after month, year after year, until he made a dent. He knocked over and over and over again until he learned the business, made connections, networked, and the wheels of his career finally started to turn. He regarded every knock as an opportunity for progress in his career, and he believed in himself so much that he got others to believe, too.

Like Billy Ray Cyrus, you first have to believe in yourself. You have to believe that you deserve wonderful memories in your life, and that you have something to offer others. Everyone has so much to give to other people, *Success Within* just helps you find and channel your unique and specific gifts. You also have to want to embrace exciting experiences, and you have to be open to change. *Success Within* provides the ideas. It is up to you to facilitate them, and to live the experiences they offer.

Step 1: Evaluate Your Progress

Take a look at the questions above and below and realistically evaluate your progress. The questions above are generally related to the entire *Success Within* program while the questions below specifically relate to what you just completed in Part 3:

1. In Week 27, what dream did you choose to make a reality? What did you have to do to devote time to this? How many steps to goal completion did you outline? Have you achieved this dream yet? Why or why not?

2. Did you make a dent in your quest for fitness in Week 28? If not, determine what is blocking your advancement in that area and try again. Believe in yourself. Believe that you really can become fit, and convince yourself of the importance of your health.

3. What fun fitness activities did you try or expand upon? Have you modified your diet? If so, what specific changes did you make?

4. How about debt? Since Week 29, have you made progress in getting out of debt or in starting a nest egg? If so, what steps did you take to accomplish this? This is a hard one and you may need more doses of Dave Ramsey's philosophy. If so, go back and check it out. Remember cash is king and debt is dumb. Cash is king and debt is dumb. Cash is. . .

5. In Week 30, which cause did you find to champion? What are you doing to assist this group or organization?

How have your efforts helped so far? Volunteering is a very important concept, and you will find happiness in sharing your talents.

6. Have you recommitted to anything, as discussed in Week 31? If so, what? How has your recommitment changed your life? How is your dedication now different from earlier times in your life? Know that in recommitment, you will find strength in your resolve. If you have fallen by the wayside in recommitment, remember to try, try again.

7. What thing did you choose to let go of in Week 32? How have you chosen to use that experience in a positive way?

8. In Week 33, how many people did you discover who were helpful to you? How were you able to thank them? What were some of the unexpected things you found to appreciate? Was there a theme to your biggest blessings of the day?

9. Did Week 34 make you reassess your honesty? How did other's opinions of you differ from your own? Through this exercise, what areas of your personality, if any, have you chosen to look at?

10. Have you solved the problem of the generation gap yet? That might be a little ambitious, but on a personal level hopefully Week 35 helped you make strides in that direction. Did you get to know an older or a younger generation? What was the most important thing you learned from them? What interests or activities did you find that you could share?

11. In Week 36, how many new things did you learn? Which was the most surprising? What piece of knowledge have you best been able to use? How were you able to pass some of your new-found knowledge along?

12. What subject or area did you decide to focus on in Week 37? What did you use to motivate yourself? Have you come closer to achieving this goal since you have focused on it? Why or why not?

13. In Week 38, in which area are you, or will you be, an expert? How, specifically, did you learn more about your subject? Who have you chosen to pass knowledge along to? Know that in sharing information you are creating a shared experience—a bond ever so slight—that might just be the beginnings of a stronger relationship.

Week 39 Success Plan

* Assess your progress with *Success Within* in general
* Evaluate the last twelve weeks to see if you have received full benefit
* Determine if there are areas that you should explore further

4

BONUS ROUND

If you have worked your way from Week 1 to this point, you have come an incredibly long way! Congratulations. Even if you have not done *Success Within* straight through, and just picked out a few weeks here and there, you will have many new and memorable moments to tell your grandchildren about. You also should be feeling great, so take time to acknowledge the many new successes in your life. Part 4, the Bonus Round, continues to provide you with a lot of fun activities that can potentially present life-changing moments. From reading and mentoring, to following through, life continues to get better and better.

Week 40

BUILDING CHARACTER

"Character is doing the right thing when nobody's looking."
—J.C. Watts

There is a huge difference between being a character and having character. Being a character means you are great at sitting on the porch and telling tall tales. Having character means your actions show moral and ethical soundness. It's acting with integrity and honor; doing the right thing instead of the easy thing.

Here is a question to ponder. If you had to define yourself in one word today, right now, what would that word be? Think about it and be honest with yourself. Now think about the connotation of the word. Is the word positive—one that would make others look up to you? Or does the word leave a bit to be desired? If the word you chose is positive, chances are you have a great deal of character. If not, then this is a week that will be especially helpful to you.

Not everyone has character. In fact, many of us don't. We tend to do what is easiest for us short-term, rather then what is best for us long-term. If you know you are supposed to pick up your sister at the airport but end up an hour late because you wanted to spend another few minutes with your friends, you took the easy way. You selfishly thought about you, and did not consider that your sister might be wasting a lot of energy worrying because you were late. Or maybe your sister is exhausted and wanted nothing more than a warm bath and a cup of tea, yet you made her sit there alone and tired in the baggage area while you had a few extra minutes of fun. How would you feel if the roles were reversed? Having character often means thinking of others more than you do yourself.

In the mid-1990s, at the height of his career, Garth Brooks showed up unannounced at Fan Fair to sign autographs. Most celebrities devote one to three hours a day once or twice during the week for autographs. When Garth showed up unannounced—and word spread that he was there—his line of fans quickly stretched to several blocks. Not wanting to disappoint anyone who waited hours to meet him, Garth signed until every fan had an autograph. The signing marathon lasted through the night and well into the next morning. When all was said and done, Garth had stood there twenty-four hours and greeted every fan with a smile on his face.

Garth Brooks showed enormous character that day. He did the right thing when the easy thing would have been to walk away after a few hours—when his legs got tired of standing and the smile on his face became stretched and tight. When it cooled off at night and the bugs came out, when his eyes began to ache from the strain, when he was so tired that he couldn't remember how to spell the name John, even though a fan with that name was standing right in front of him and had spelled it three times, Garth could have left. His fans would have been disappointed, but everyone knows that the celebrities have tight schedules to keep. But Garth wasn't thinking of his tired legs or aching eyes. He knew how much it meant to his fans to meet him, so he stayed the course. Garth Brooks has character.

How many times have you walked away from a tough situation? We all have at one time or another, both in relationships and at work. But having character means that you do not walk away from a situation lightly. It means you put others before yourself, and you consider the full consequences of your actions to everyone concerned—before you act. You try your best to do the best for everyone involved, even at your own expense.

Try taking a guess at the number of people who rely on you for anything, large or small. If you make a quick list and see it in front of you in black and white you might be surprised at the number of people you impact. I once wrote a story about a rural Meals-on-Wheels program. One of the recipients of those meals told me that even though she was frail and in her nineties, she just had to stay healthy because the woman who delivered lunch to her every day was having a tough time in her marriage and needed to see a smiling face. This aged woman knew her delivery person drew strength from the simple sight of an elderly, quavering smile. So the next time you think about walking away from someone or something, know that the smallest role you play in the life of another could be very important to them.

This week you will determine just how much character you have, and how to make the most of it.

Step 1: Being a Character or Having it?

There is nothing wrong with being a character, as long as you back it up by having character. Here are a few questions to ask yourself about character.

1. Who is your number one hero and what qualities do they possess that made you choose them?

2. Would you allow your face to be severely disfigured if it guaranteed you would live a healthy life for at least one hundred years? Before answering, put yourself into the shoes you might wear if you went through life with a major facial deformity. Consider the aspects of discrimination in the job market, how this would affect personal relationships, and the psychological impact of strangers perpetually talking to your shoulder or forehead, instead of looking at your face.

3. Now turn the tables. If the person you planned to spend the rest of your life with had an accident that caused horrible scars on their face, would you continue with your plans of a lifetime together, or would you back out? Why or why not?

4. If you could choose to hurt anyone in the world with words, who would it be and what would you say to them? Would the words be to a person who once hurt you in some way? Would saying the words make you feel any better?

5. Would you kill an innocent stranger if you knew that in doing so a cure for AIDS or another disease would be found? Why or why not? Consider all the lives that would be saved through the cure versus the value one stranger might bring to the world. Consider that this stranger might be the next Beethoven or rocket scientist. If allowed to live, he or she could be the father or mother of someone who does something even better for the world than finding a cure for AIDS. Then again, how valuable would it be to the world for everyone who lives a life shortened by illness or disease to live a full

life? What positives might those people bring to society?

6. If your friends decided to do something that you did not think was a good idea, would you do it with them? Why or why not? Would you try to talk your friends out of it?

7. What kinds of requests do you find hard to say no to—requests you invariably wish you hadn't agreed to? If you later regret it, why do you say yes? Is it because you want to be liked, you need money, you don't think everything through, or . . .?

8. If you knew for certain that the world would end one year from today, how would you live out the year?

Step 2: You Are the Company You Keep

When my son was in kindergarten, he became friends with a boy I'll call Freddy. Freddy was one of these kids who found trouble every time he turned around. Freddy wasn't really looking for trouble—he just automatically attracted it. Several times my son, by way of being Freddy's friend, also got in trouble. It was more trouble by association than actual wrong doing on my son's part, but it brought the lesson home that you really are the company you keep.

If you are striving to act with character, it becomes very hard if you surround yourself with those who don't have any. If people around you are acting selfishly and without honor, then it becomes very easy for you to act that way as well. Some people are like Freddy; they try to do the right thing. Even though it often does not work out that way, their intentions were good. Other people just do not care.

This week take time to evaluate the character of all the

people in your inner circle. This would include your family, close friends, co-workers, fellow students, and anyone else whom you are around regularly. If you are having difficulty doing what's right, it might be because the people around you are taking the easy route rather than the right one.

Now look at your list again and determine the people with whom you spend most of your free time. Do these people act with character? Are they people you trust?

Step 3: Commit to Character
Based on steps one and two, decide if you need to make any changes in your personal relationships. If the people you are most often with at work or at school, at social clubs or at church, are lacking in the character department, you might consider looking for people who live their lives with a little more integrity. Who knows why a person might be selfish, unreliable or untrustworthy, but that is for that individual to work out. You don't want to disown or shun these people who have been in your life, but do consider choosing to spend more time with people you can look up to and people whom you admire.

Week 40 Success Plan

* Determine if you are a character or whether you have character
* Evaluate the character of your inner circle
* Think about the types of people you choose to spend free time with
* Commit to a gradual shift and spend more time with those you admire

Week 41

WORKING HARD
OR HARDLY WORKING?

"The harder you work, the luckier you get."
—Gary Player

Today, more than ever, we have thousands of stimuli that pull at our attention. Every day we have hundreds of choices of television programs or movies to watch. There are numerous phone calls and emails that consume our time. Many people are juggling kids, school, housework, lawn maintenance, business meetings, exercise, financial difficulties, health issues, extended family, and oh, did you say you wanted a life, too?

I often find myself drifting off my planned course for the day. I may have forty-seven things I have to do—many of which only take a minute or two—but then find I have spent an hour on the phone with an old friend who called out of the blue. Or my computer crashed and I have to re-boot three times. There just went another twenty minutes. Then a client needs something from me that I hadn't counted on doing that day. There's another half an hour gone. Before I know it, it's midnight and I still have work left.

If you want to enjoy an orderly life where you accomplish your daily goals *and* have ample personal time, it is important to make good use of your time. Many of my clients can attest to that fact as they have dozens of items on their plate each and every day. Even so, they often grimace when I give them their schedules for the media days we plan every few months. For media days, I actually plan their itinerary in fifteen-minute increments, sometimes starting as early as six in the morning. I even scheduled their PBs (potty breaks). I am sure at times they think I am the publicist from hell, but I know we have a lot to accomplish on those days and a limited amount of time to get it done. Additionally, I know if there is the least bit of slack in the itinerary, we will stray off course and fall behind. If, for example, we have an extra fifteen minutes my client might want to make a quick run to a nearby clothing store or a coffee shop. Then, of course, the fifteen minutes ends up being at least three times that long and we miss several interviews.

Everyone wastes some time during the day. That's reality. Sometimes I just have to ignore the email and phones and go out for a walk or sit for a few minutes on the porch. But I use that quiet time to refocus so I can accomplish the rest of what I need to do that day.

Real success—in any area of your life—involves hard work. But the secret to accomplishing your goals is not in working hard. It is in working smart. That means you are making the best possible use of your time and skills. Different people are good at different activities, and everyone has a unique set of strengths and weaknesses. You just have to know what yours are and learn to delegate what you can.

It is frustrating and overwhelming to be so overloaded with commitments that you miss deadlines and forget to do important tasks. You let others down and disappoint yourself. When I find myself in that position, the only way I can dig myself out is to focus on one small item at a time until I can pull myself out far enough to see the rest of my life.

Then, once you've gotten to the point where you can focus, things begin to get done.

It also helps if you know one simple two-letter word. No. Sometimes you just need to say it. I wear many hats, but if I have too much to do, nothing gets done. I have learned that even though I want to, I can't do everything and I can't please everyone.

This week you will evaluate your day and learn to find more time by doing away with a few tasks, streamlining some and delegating others. You will learn to work smart so you have more time to find great moments with family and friends.

Step 1: Evaluate Your Day

Every day this week, record everything you do and how long it takes you to do it. You might want to record all of this in your *Success Within* notebook, or create some other system where it is easy for you to keep all the information in one spot. More than likely, even if you are a very busy person, you will be quite surprised at the amount of time you really spend doing nothing, or the long amount of time it takes to do relatively unimportant activities throughout the day.

Step 2: Make More Time

At some point every day, take a very good look at how you are really spending your time. Once you have a true understanding of the length of time you spend at different tasks, you can begin to streamline. If you vacuum and then take a walk, try putting on some high-powered music and give yourself a workout while you vacuum instead. That's probably a good ten minutes saved right there. Consider whether you really need to wash the car three times a week. How much time does that really take? Unless it is also a good bonding time with another family member, you might consider washing the car only once a week. Or, if you are always running to the store, plan ahead and decide you are only going two or three times a week. If you forget something, you'll just do without. The world will not end if you are without bread for a day or two.

Now think about how much time you can save if you find an easier, and quicker, way. Does it really take a full hour to get ready for work? Think about what you can do to combine tasks and save ten to fifteen minutes. Can you do some of it the night before? Is your hairstyle so high-maintenance that it takes half an hour just to do your hair? Is it worth spending all that time with a brush and a blow dryer?

The last part of this exercise involves delegating everything you absolutely do not have to do yourself. Isn't your ten-year-old, old enough to start doing some of her own laundry? Shouldn't you teach your assistant to help with some of your lower-level responsibilities? Or, if *you* are the assistant, can you find an intern or receptionist you can teach to do one of your tasks? It's not passing the buck. It's clearing the cobwebs out of your life so you can be even more productive. As you go through this process, you will find that by delegating, you are making those around you more responsible. Sure, people might gripe and complain at first, but you are teaching those you delegate to new career and life skills, and making each person a more resourceful individual. They will thank you—eventually.

Be relentless. Find tasks you can do less often, figure out ways to combine errands and chores, and recruit those you live or work with to get off their butts and help out.

Step 3: Evaluate Your Strengths and Weaknesses

Let's face it. I am not a good cook. I don't even boil water well. When I was in college it only took two days before my roommates banned me from turning on the stove. And later, I inadvertently set my own kitchen on fire so many times that I ended up dating one of the firemen. The dispatcher begged me to call the station when I got hungry, saying it would be cheaper for the county to have a pizza delivered to my house than to send out the fire trucks every other day. It is fair to say that cooking is not one of my strengths. On the other hand, I am good with horses and kids and in motivating people. To be most effective, I have had to find ways to minimize my involvement in the kitchen, and maximize the time I spend in my stronger areas.

You, too, have strengths and weaknesses and it is time to figure out exactly what they are. You know what you are good at, so write down all the areas in which you excel. You also know what you aren't effective at. Remember, these are not lists of what you like or don't like. You should list both your strong and weak areas, regardless of how well you like or dislike them. Maybe you are good with your hands: carpentry, woodworking, and repair, but organization and math are not your strong points. See if you can delegate any accounting or bill paying chores in exchange for increased maintenance responsibilities around your home or job. Just because someone has always had a certain area of responsibility does not mean that it is the best area of responsibility for that person, and you might be pleasantly surprised at the positive reaction people have when you bring up the possibility of swapping duties.

Step 4: Enjoy Your New Found Freedom
As you go through the week you will find yourself changing the activities in your life. Be prepared for a little chaos before settling into a new routine. Also, you will likely find some extra time on your hands. Just think of all the ways you can spend it! You can spend time with your loved ones, learn a new skill, take a walk, sit on the porch and watch the birds, or even take a much needed nap.

Week 41 Success Plan

* Record how you spend your time throughout the day
* Combine tasks, eliminate unnecessary chores, and delegate
* Restructure your life to build on your strengths and weaknesses
* Enjoy your extra time

Week 42

ACTS OF CONSIDERATION

"A little Consideration, a little Thought for Others, makes all the difference." —Winnie the Pooh

It is human nature to want to be first in line, to have the most, to accomplish more than anyone else. But in this me-me-me-world, hogging all the fun and glory is not considerate of others. And not being considerate eliminates the chance for wonderful things to circle back to you.

Bill Vandiver understands that principle well. Bill is a hair stylist and co-owns The Edge of Belle Meade salon in Nashville. He is much in demand throughout the year, but during the year-end holidays he spends time giving back in unexpected ways.

One year on Christmas Eve, Bill and a friend met at a restaurant for afternoon coffee and pie. "I felt really sorry for the waiters and waitresses who had to work on Christmas Eve," Bill told me. "I'm sure they would rather be home with their kids and families. My thinking is that if they are working on Christmas Eve, they *really* need the money."

When he left, Bill gave his waitress a one hundred dollar tip. She was so overwhelmed with Bill's generosity that she began to cry and told him she had been praying for a large tip so she could do some last minute Christmas shopping for her kids.

That one incident began a tradition for Bill. Now every year on or around Christmas Eve, Bill and several friends make an afternoon of visiting as many restaurants as they can manage. They fill themselves with coffee and conversation and pie, and when they leave, each person who waited on them receives a generous tip.

"It's one way that I have of giving back," says Bill. "If I was waiting tables around Christmas time, I know I'd like someone to do that for me, and it makes me really happy to do that for them."

Somehow, Bill knew exactly what his waitress needed. He considered that need and provided it. The difference in a general act of kindness and in one of consideration is that you really have to give a lot of thought (or consideration) to a specific need of a specific person. A general act of kindness might mean opening a door for a woman loaded down with packages. An act of consideration would mean providing a door for a retiree who really needed one.

After the first season of the hit television show, *The Apprentice*, Donald Trump offered to pay college tuition fees for one of the candidates. That one person, Troy McClain, had been unable to pursue a college education due to family commitments. Donald Trump considered this specific need for this specific person, and offered to provide it.

Surely someone in your world needs something. When my son was about a year old I got a job doing editing and graphic design for a small city-book publisher. I am a bit nearsighted and was having trouble making the drive to work, as I did not have any glasses. Even the simplest pair was way out of my price range. My employer kindly offered to pay for my eye exam and glasses, for which I will be forever grateful. It not only made my life much easier, but also much safer.

A year prior to that, just after my son was born, an anonymous person dropped off a huge bag of groceries the day before Thanksgiving. Without that thoughtful generosity, we would have been eating jelly sandwiches for Thanksgiving dinner.

Acts of consideration are often very small things to the giver and very big things to the recipient. Acts of consideration help provide the most basic needs in life. The Twilight Wish Foundation is a small charitable organization that specializes in granting specific wishes for seniors. The first wish they granted was to provide a grave marker for the deceased son of an elderly woman who could not afford to buy her son a headstone. Since then they have provided many simple wishes for elderly people. These acts of consideration make life easier and give peace of mind.

I have a friend who wishes to remain anonymous, but she and a group of her friends learned of a young single mother who was trying to pull her way out of poverty. They took turns watching her two young children while she took night classes to earn her GED. Then they took her to a consignment store and spent thirty dollars to buy her two outfits that she could wear for interviews. That small group of women totally changed that young mother's life, and the life of her children.

Acts of consideration do not need to involve money or a lot of time. You could provide a ride to work for someone in your church who is having transportation problems. You could cook and deliver a meal to a neighbor who is ill. You could offer to fix a window for an elderly person, or mow the lawn, or hang a curtain. The ideas are endless and are dictated only by the needs of the recipient.

Step 1: Identify a Need

There are people in need all around you. It might be a family member or a neighbor, or a friend of a friend. If you can't spot a person in need right away, ask your friends, people at church, local social groups, your neighbors, or your relatives if they know of anyone—young or old—who is in need of some simple something that would improve his or her life. Before too long you should have a list of people whose lives could easily be improved by an act of consideration.

Step 2: Ask the Recipient

Just because you or someone else feels that old Mrs. Peterson's house needs to be painted, does not mean that *she* thinks it does. It is very important that you obtain the permission of the recipient before you provide your act of consideration. Often, by talking with a person in need, you will find that there are other items that are far more needed, than what you had originally planned. It doesn't help to give a needy neighbor a side of beef if he doesn't have a freezer in which to store it.

Step 3: Be Realistic

If a man who is living in poverty needs to visit a dying parent on the other side of the country, it is not necessary for you to provide the means for that trip. If you have a way to do it without straining your finances, then go right ahead. But if not, then tell him that if he can find a way to get the air or bus fare, that you will take him to the airport or bus station and look in on his apartment while he is away.

Step 4: Do it Now

If you promise to do something, then do it. There is nothing more disappointing to the recipient of a considerate act than one that is promised, but not delivered. Keep in mind that a ride to Wal-Mart can be a big event for some people. Vacuuming a living room for a woman who has allergies or is recuperating from surgery can mean the difference between staying well and getting sick. If you agree to do it, then do it. It might be a little matter to you, but keep in mind that it can be a very big deal to the person you are helping.

Step 5: Watch Them Smile

There is nothing more rewarding than putting a smile on someone's face. That smile can be so empowering that you will remember it for the rest of your life. It will be so memorable, that it will make you want to go out and perform other acts of consideration. You can even share that wonderful feeling you now have with others, by encouraging them to help a person in need.

Week 42 Success Plan

* Find someone who needs a specific thing
* Obtain their consent
* Be realistic in what you can do
* Be timely in your delivery
* Enjoy all the smiles that are coming your way

EMBRACE CHANGE

"If nothing ever changed, there'd be no butterflies."
—Anonymous

Change is good. Sometimes it is hard and, often it is very different, but embracing change—inevitable change—is much easier to do than fighting it.

There used to be a television talk show called *Miller & Company*, hosted by Dan Miller, who is now a Nashville news anchor. The show combined wonderful in-depth interviews of artists with casual, acoustic performances. One of my clients at the time the show was running was Marty Haggard (the oldest son of the legendary Merle Haggard) and I had the opportunity to book Marty, Merle, and Marty's brother, Noel Haggard, on the show. This was one of the very few times all three ever appeared together on television, and the show's entire staff was very excited.

About noon on the day the show was to tape, one of the producers called my office to be sure the limo had picked up all three of the Haggard men. I confirmed the three were on their way and headed in my own car to the studio. Imagine my shock when I got to the studio to find that between the time the producer called and the fifteen minutes it took me to get to the studio, the network had called and cancelled the show. And, as is typical in television, once you are cancelled, you are cancelled. Everything stops immediately. The network, however, agreed to run the Haggard show as a special encore edition, but everyone on staff was in tears throughout the taping.

What it boiled down to was that everyone was sad because the life each staff member liked so well and was currently living was going to change drastically. To make the situation worse, no one had any choice in the matter. Everyone was in shock, and as yet unable to accept this change.

There is a lot of uncertainty and fear anytime there are major changes in life. In the case of the staff of *Miller & Company,* many were worried about their financial status and were wondering how he or she would pay their bills. One man wondered how long it would be before he could find a new job, and whether it would be in television, a medium he loved, but one in which opportunities were limited in Nashville. Another was very sad that the friendships she had on the set would naturally end over time and drift apart. All were disappointed that, for whatever reason, ratings were not high enough to warrant the network placing more faith in the show, and each person took the cancellation as a personal affront to their professional capabilities. Additionally, it all came as a huge surprise, so no one was prepared to deal with this sudden crisis.

Change is inevitable. Unless you are a cast member in the movie *Groundhog Day,* the Bill Murray movie where everyone wakes up only to begin the previous day all over again, you will have some changes in your life every single day. No day is exactly the same as the one before it, even if you follow the same basic routine. Life is really just a series of changes. Plants and flowers grow, trees mature, and the shorelines of lakes and rivers change ever so slightly from day to day. Why, even our bodies change somewhat from one day to the next.

When I was young, there was a very nice swing set in our yard. In the summers when I was small, I remember spending a lot of time there and finding a lot of enjoyment in it. But as I grew older, other interests took my time and I spent less and less time swinging and sliding down the little slide. Then, when I was in college, the swing set was sold. Of course, I was horrified. Not having the swing set changed the look of our yard dramatically. There was, to my eyes, a huge empty, open spot. I loved that swing set. From my perspective, it didn't matter that I hadn't used it in many years. I loved it, and felt it belonged in our yard.

Over time, I overcame the shock. I was able to see that the swing set was much better off being used by other children who hopefully enjoyed it as much as I did. It was not being used or maintained when it was in our yard and would soon have become nothing more than a pile of scrap metal. I can now see that the change was not only necessary, it was good.

Although this could certainly be classified as a minor event in just about anyone's life, it taught me a lot about accepting change—and embracing it.

Making any change, whether it is a business or personal change, can be difficult. Some changes we can choose and control, many others we cannot. Some are huge changes such as marriage or divorce, birth or death, while others are very small changes in our daily lives, yet nonetheless they affect us dramatically.

Think of this: Many of the small everyday activities we do can be considered a kind of tradition. You "traditionally" get up at a certain time every day. You may traditionally have specific foods for breakfast, leave for work at a certain time, and so on throughout your day. These are all things that become familiar to us and that we become comfortable with. Any change in those routines—or traditions—can be stressful. But the changes can also be good and improve our lives over the long-term.

In addition to our traditional daily routines, much of what we hold on to the hardest in our lives involves time-honored family traditions that are passed down from one generation to the next. Sadly, these wonderful traditions are becoming increasingly hard to maintain in our new global world. Families who live thousands of miles apart can no longer get together every holiday. Young couples often split holidays between two families, so one family is always missing a daughter or a son on any given occasion.

This week you will examine some of the changes you've fought in your life, and ways you can develop new traditions around those—and other—changes. New traditions will bring wonderful new memories to mix with sweet remembrances of the old. And instead of fighting change you will learn to welcome it as a new and exciting chapter in your life.

Step 1: Examine Big Changes

Look back and identify the three biggest changes in your life—the three events that had the biggest impact on you. For me, one of them was when a mare I had in training fell and landed on my knee, ending my professional riding career. It was a terrible time and I felt as if my lifelong dream of working with horses had been taken from me. At the time, and for years after, I fought the reality of my injury in many, many ways. But, had it not happened, I would never have moved to Nashville, never would have had my many amazing experiences in the entertainment industry, and ultimately would never have written this book. Even though I still deal with knee problems on a daily basis, I am very glad life turned out the way it did, because I wouldn't trade the people I have met or experiences I have had for anything.

When you think about it, you probably have quite a few events that have significantly changed your life, but for now, we will just concentrate on three. It may take you a few days to sort through your memories and realize the events that were the biggest catalysts for change. Thinking back and having the perspective of time, was each change something you sought, or was it out of your control? Was each change ultimately good for you? Did it cause you to have new experiences in your life or to meet people you otherwise would not have met? Did you learn anything from the change? And, if you fought the change at the time, would it have been easier if you had accepted it and moved on with your life? If you consider these questions whenever change hits you smack in the face in the future, hopefully you will see the amazing possibilities change can bring, rather than fearing the unknown.

Step 2: Recognize Your Traditions
Everyone has traditions in their life that they love, and some they could do without! When I first moved to Nashville we moved around a lot, so now once a year my son and I—not on any specific day but traditionally around the holidays—take a drive and visit all the places we used to live. It is a way for us to reconnect with our past and revisit some great

memories. Paul Overstreet and his family traditionally hold a baseball game in their backyard on Mother's Day, and invite their many friends, along with their families, to participate and enjoy the fun. On Thanksgiving, another friend and her family make lists of the five things each are individually most thankful for. Every year they place their lists in the family Bible, and my friend gets great enjoyment in looking over lists from years past.

Make time this week to take stock of the traditions that are the most vital to you and decide just why these specific traditions are important in your life. You may wish to share your thoughts with your family, or close friends. Usually, even if people do not share your enthusiasm, once it is understood why the tradition is important to you, they are more willing to be a part of it.

Step 3: Begin a New Tradition

Also this week, take a moment to identify traditions that no longer work for you or your family. You may—individually or with the consent of the others who share the tradition—wish to modify the tradition, or discard it entirely. But, know that it is important to get an okay from everyone involved if you want to make changes to any time-honored family traditions. Just because the tradition is not important to you does not mean it doesn't have meaning for another person. If you need to understand further why the tradition is important to someone else, by all means, ask! His or her explanation may change your mind. If a tradition is just not working, be sure to explain your perspective clearly and concisely, and remember that while you have given this idea some serious thought, it will be a brand new concept to the people who share it with you. Initially, they may not be as receptive to the idea as you are. Be open and allow for their feedback.

If you discard a tradition completely, try to come up with a new tradition to take its place. All old traditions got their start somewhere. Maybe someday your new ideas for a family (or work) tradition will be considered timeless and "old."

Week 43 Success Plan

* Examine the three biggest three changes in your life
* Learn to embrace changes in the future
* Recognize the traditions most important to you
* Modify traditions that no longer work for you or your family
* Begin new traditions to replace the old

Week 44

MENTOR ANOTHER

"Mentoring is a brain to pick, an ear to listen, and a push in the right direction." —John Crosby

Other than fame, what do Olympic skaters Viktor Petrenko and Oksana Baiul, *All in the Family* star Carroll O'Connor and Larry Hagman of *Dallas*, and superstars Tina Turner and Mick Jagger all have in common? Give up? They are three well-known mentor pairs, the first name in the pair having helped the second learn the ropes of their respective careers, and assisted in it whenever possible.

These wise people know there is nothing more rewarding than watching someone you've helped go on to accomplish fantastic things with his or her life. But you do not have to be a celebrity to be a mentor. Whether it is a grandchild, a younger sibling, a virtual stranger, or the new kid at the office, serving as a mentor can be one of the biggest thrills of your life.

So what exactly is a mentor? A mentor is a person who takes an active interest in another, and who acts as their trusted counselor, advisor, or guide. Some mentors are spiritual guides, others are people who are leaders in their chosen field and who are willing to pull another person up the career ladder with them. Yet other mentors are sports coaches, older relatives, or teachers—basically anyone who can open a few doors for you in life and who can also help you walk through them.

The original Mentor is thought by many to be a fictional character in a poem involving Greek mythology called *The Odyssey*. *The Odyssey* originated around 800 B.C. and the original story, which is attributed to a man named Homer, would have been told orally, rather than written. In any case, it is a wonderful, magical tale about Odysseus, the King of Ithaca. When Odysseus left Ithaca to fight in the Trojan War, he entrusted his kingdom to a man who, aptly, was named Mentor. While Odysseus was away, Mentor also served as a teacher to Odysseus's son. Since then, anyone who guides another along life's path has been called a mentor.

We talk a lot these days about heroes and role models––who all too often end up being actors, athletes, or pop or rock stars. But those who are closest to us, those we can see up close and in person, are the ones who really influence us the most. Rather than admiring from afar, mentoring involves a very personal one-on-one relationship. And the best part about all of this is that mentoring is as much a learning experience for the mentor as it is for the one being mentored. Know that in the long run you, as a mentor, are going to get far more out of the whole process than you put in.

It's also important to realize that mentors do not need to have all the answers, so do not let that intimidate you. Anyone can be a mentor, because everyone has some knowledge and perspective to give. The mentoring relationship works simply because mentors are helping others. Those being mentored know the mentor is taking a personal interest, and that makes all the difference in the world because it makes them feel special.

Mentoring can take up a little bit of your time, or a lot. It can be a short-term proposition that lasts a few weeks, or an intricate relationship that lasts a lifetime. It is your choice. You decide how much time and knowledge you can afford to give. There is no real formula to being a mentor, other than committing to being be an advisor to someone in a certain area. Every mentoring relationship is different and takes on a life of its own. Here are a few ideas to get you started.

Step 1: Establish Your Parameters

As stated earlier, mentoring can be an occasional effort, or more involved and rewarding. Either works. But before you find a person to mentor, you need to take stock of your own life. In what areas do you feel you can be beneficial to another person? Education, career, family, sports, hobby, and relationships are just a few areas to consider. Are you great with kids or do you prefer to work with adults? If you'd rather work with adults, are there some bright, young stars at your office or in your trade organization? Do you enjoy reading and the educational process, or are you more of a hands-on do-it-yourself kind of person? And lastly, how much time do you have to put toward this project? Put the answers to these questions together and you will begin to get an idea of where you can be the most beneficial in the mentoring process.

Step 2: Find Someone to Mentor

Now that you have an idea of where you want to go with this, you need to find someone you can help along the way. If you are thinking long-term and kids, there are many options. The Big Brother and Big Sister organizations are great if you want to help a child who needs a role model.

Churches, social service organizations, and high school counselors are also good sources if you are looking to mentor a young person.

If you enjoy teaching, these same organizations will know of an adult who can't read, or who needs help studying for a GED, or assistance in getting their foot in the door for a job interview. Sometimes people just need another person to care and believe in them while they try to improve their lives. Others need the encouraging push that a mentor can provide.

Maybe you excel (or excelled at one time) at a specific hobby, talent or sport and can help a younger person with natural raw ability to understand the ins and outs of that specific skill set or industry.

If you are more career oriented and don't have as much time, find a real go-getter at your office—someone who needs a little help with introductions to the real movers and shakers in your industry. Giving that person a little help now may pay off in many ways for you down the road. You can also contact a Small Business Association office or the chamber of commerce in your area. They are both great at people-to-people connections and should be very supportive of your desire to mentor.

It is also entirely possible to mentor a member of your own family. Do you have a younger brother or sister who needs a little extra attention? How about a niece or nephew who is getting lost in the mess of their parent's divorce? Maybe there is an adult grandchild who needs some direction or encouragement. With his or her consent, you can make any of these people a little more special in your life, and offer your wisdom, expertise and support while they strive to reach their own personal goals.

Step 3: Agree on the Process

Once you've found someone to mentor, sit down with him and explain what you have in mind. Explain that mentoring means you will be there when he needs you. Note that in most situations this does not mean disruptive three A.M. phone calls or knocks on your door. It means that you will, to the best of your ability, offer ideas on how he can further his education, or reach personal and career goals. You can lend perspective to life's puzzling challenges, offer advice, or introduce him to other people who can help him in all of this—you are there for him.

As you get to know the person you are mentoring a little better, your role will change and grow as he progresses through his existing goals and establishes new ones. He may come to you for support on an idea he has, an introduction, or to reach understanding on certain people or processes.

One of the great enticements in mentoring is in knowing up front that no matter how you look at it, this will be an exciting adventure for both of you. You will be able to share with a strong sense of pride his accomplishments, and know that you had a hand, however small, in making his dreams come true. Indeed, helping someone else find achievement in life is the greatest gift one person can give to another, and to his or herself. In mentoring, you are sure to find many of your greatest moments.

* Establish your strengths and evaluate your time commitment
* Find someone to mentor
* Commit to helping him or her achieve their goals in whatever way you can
* Wear your pride well—you deserve it

HAVE YOU READ
A GOOD BOOK LATELY?

*"No matter how busy you may think you are, you must find time
for reading, or surrender yourself to self-chosen ignorance."*
—Confucius

The good news is that you are a reader. I know this because you have made it all the way to Week 45. The
bad news is that every year fewer people crack open a book
than the year before. And of the books cracked open, most
are never finished. Thousands of people, for whatever reason, have never been able to find enjoyment in holding the
weight of a book in their hand. They have never discovered
the wonders of knowledge and entertainment found inside
the pages of a book. They have never known the thrill of
discovering a real page-turner, of staying up until four in the
morning because they just couldn't put the book down.

I am a firm believer that people who aren't readers just
haven't yet found the right style of book. With well over a
hundred thousand new titles to choose from each year, I believe that all it takes is a little time to find the right kind of
book, and in the right format. Even people who read very
slowly or not very well, should be able to find something.

Whenever my clients complained to me of being bored
while out on the road, I suggested a good book to read.
When a non-reader cautioned that she wasn't willing to
spend twenty dollars on something she might not like, I
asked if she was willing to spend five dollars. She agreed
that she was, so I mentioned paperbacks. Then, as soon as

she returned from her trip, I scheduled a trip to the library.

While walking rows and rows of shelves filled floor to ceiling with books excites me, I know it can be intimidating to others—especially those who find reading difficult. So I'd lead my bored clients directly to books that featured subject matter that was familiar to them: music, music history, and celebrity biographies. I would have previously selected books that were formatted with larger type sizes and lots of white on the margins to make the books look less threatening. I encouraged each client to select a few to borrow on my library card. The vast majority soon asked if we could go back for more. And we invariably did.

On the second trip, I encouraged my clients to look at books outside his or her immediate level of familiarity. One artist loved boats, so we looked at a current guide to the newer makes and models of speedboats. Another was interested in fishing, so we found a book that listed many of the best fishing spots in the Southeast. Once these people realized that books could help expand interest and improve knowledge, they suddenly became readers. And while our tastes often differed, I was thrilled that they were finding their own pleasure and enjoyment in books. A nice little side note is that once a client started reading, they were no longer bored while out on the road.

Having taken a lot of non-readers to libraries and to bookstores, I know that for the uninitiated, the vast variety of subject matter and formats available is a huge surprise. Many do not realize that a lot of libraries and bookstores also offer audio books and movies. Others do not recognize that most libraries allow you to check out materials at no charge and often for several weeks at a time.

The people I have come into contact with who do not read much associate books with bad school memories, or stressful situations involving tests or writing papers. They have not yet learned there is a wealth of fun and interesting ideas in books.

My personal love of books began very early and was nurtured by my mother and grandmother, and two librarians. When I was in the third grade, I remember how excited I was when our elementary school librarian took me all the way across the library and allowed me to check out books that only the big kids (fourth, fifth, and sixth graders) were allowed to read. And while we never had much money, my mother always scraped together enough so I could order whatever I wanted from the monthly school book club.

This week you will expand your own reading and also introduce someone else to the wonder of books.

Step 1: Step Outside Your Comfort Zone

While I personally am ecstatic that you are reading *Success Within*, this week I encourage you to step outside your comfort zone and read a book that you normally would not read.

If you are a self-help kind of person, try a novel. I love mysteries and chick-lit, while my son is more interested in thrillers and science fiction. If you are not sure what you might like, block out some time to spend at the library or your local bookstore. Browse the shelves until you find something that piques your interest. The people who work wherever books are found should also be very willing to make recommendations, based on your interests.

If you, like my son, usually enjoy science fiction, try a biography. If you regularly read business books, or books that pertain to your career, try a novel that was set in your hometown. The familiarity you have with the streets and places mentioned in the book will only add to your enchantment.

You might even have some friends or relatives who have been encouraging you to read a particular book, but for whatever reason, you just didn't think it was for you. Well now is the time. In addition to experiencing a new book, you will make the person who recommended the book feel great. And, it is good to remember that a lively discussion about a book can lead to great insight about yourself and the other person. So if he or she is important to you in some way, the promise of great conversation can be a nice incentive.

This week may be the beginning of a fabulous new chapter in your life, one featuring great happiness as you discover new authors and genres of books that, for one reason or another, speak to you. And remember, if at first you do not succeed, try, try again. There are many genres of books and writing styles, and you are sure to discover some that you really enjoy. But if, after you have tried several, you find that printed words just do not work for you, try audio books. They are a great solution, especially if you have poor vision or if you have a neurological problem that causes your head or hands to shake.

Step 2: Turn Someone On
If you are like me, you probably know more people who don't read than those who do. This week, in addition to ex-

panding your own reading horizons, you will be on a mission to gently introduce people to the world of books.

Maybe you have a very young person in your life who would enjoy going to a story hour at a library or bookstore. When my son was about three, I took him to the eleven o'clock story hour at Davis-Kidd booksellers without fail every Saturday for the better part of a year. He loved it, and I found that I did, too. From the moment Colby was born, I was reading to him, and I believe that reading a story from a book at a specific time of day, such as bedtime, is a fun, comforting routine for both parent and child.

Older children, and adults who are not readers, may be more hesitant due to stressful experiences with school and books. You will just have to search to find their hot spot. What turns this person on? Is it racecars, or ponies, or mystical adventures, or history, or kites? What about guitars, rock stars, home remodeling, crafts, investing, or fashion? No matter what he or she is interested in, there are books on that subject at a reading level perfect for each of them.

You may have to start slow. Ask if he will accompany you while you go to a library or bookstore. While you are there, ask his opinion about different books and introduce the idea of actually taking a book home. You will not make a reader out of him overnight, but over time, he could become an avid book lover.

Another idea is to talk in casual conversation to him about a book you have read. If you have been discussing an upcoming holiday, you could merge into a funny story about a holiday in a book you just read.

It is possible that you even know someone who is functionally illiterate. While this could be a big challenge for you, think of the gift you would be giving this person if you could teach him or her, or arrange to have them taught, to read. Think how much easier their life would be. Can you imagine not being able to comprehend the words in newspapers, on nutrition labels of food packages, and on job applications? You would completely rewrite the story of their life if you had a hand in teaching them to read. And, what a wonder to reflect upon in your later years: the fact that you turned a person who couldn't read into a book lover, and changed a life because of it.

Week 45 Success Plan

* Expand your horizons by reading a type of book that is new to you
* If you do not enjoy that book, try another style or genre
* Turn someone on to the wonderful world of books
* Go slowly and be patient. Over time you could significantly change his or her life

Week 46

TAKE A PAGE FROM MACGYVER

"Life is a continuous exercise in creative problem solving."
—Michael J. Gelb

Remember the television show *MacGyver*? He's the guy who could create a bomb with a chocolate bar and a wad of gum, and reroute an electric grid with a couple of keystrokes. This week's plan doesn't go quite that far, but it is all about making something from nothing.

When I was ten or eleven, we had a school exercise where we had to list all the uses we could think of for a nail. Most kids came up with about fifteen uses; I listed over one hundred. Once I got in the mindset, I could not stop the ideas from flowing. A few of the uses I listed included using a nail to write an SOS message in the dirt, pounding a series of large nails part-way into a tree trunk to create a ladder to a tree house, using a nail to stir coffee or tea, and tying a long string to two nails to mark off a straight section for a fence.

The basic idea of the exercise was two-fold. One was to find practical uses for everyday items, and the other was to reuse items we might otherwise throw away. Since then, I have been very conscious of both and take special note when I see something being used in an unusual way.

For example, in the entertainment industry, celebrities often spread a thin layer of the hemorrhoid ointment Preparation H around their eyes to tighten nature's droops and folds before an interview or photo shoot. Hair clips are used in photo and video shoots to make the star's clothes fit more snugly. If you saw the backside of a celebrity during one of these shoots, you would likely see a half a dozen of these clips placed very strategically. Hair spray is also used on the body to keep clothes from shifting. Sometimes, a thin layer of Vaseline is used on teeth to keep lips from sticking during interviews, and the ever popular duct tape can be utilized to stretch, pull and mold certain body parts into more interesting forms. Male stars often use mascara or shoe polish to temporarily darken beards that are beginning to gray, and guitar players have been known to use a small triangular piece of an old credit card in lieu of a guitar pick.

No matter what it is that you do, you can probably find a number of uses for items you usually throw away. Shredded paper makes great packing material inside boxes. An old pair of pantyhose is great for tying up tomatoes, peonies, and other plants that tend to weigh themselves down.

The theme for this week is creative thinking as you find innovative ways to use items around your home or office, instead of buying something specifically for that purpose.

Step 1: Take Creative Stock

Depending on the size of your living space, block an hour or an evening this week to look around and gather the odds and ends around your home. Look for possessions you haven't used in more than a year, or items you were planning to throw out. Find a place where you can sort through the bits and pieces, and as you do, look for things that can be used in a new way within your home or office. One of the best sets of curtains I ever had I made from an old lace tablecloth that had one tear too many to use on the table, but could be mended well enough to look great as a window treatment. Do you have any old lawnmower parts or tools that can be grouped attractively in your yard as a piece of garden art, or a rusted wheelbarrow that can be turned into a planter?

This gathering and sorting process can be a great way to involve your entire family. But don't stop there. You can make a group or even a neighborhood project out of turning some of the rescued items into something that is usable in other ways. Let your children or grandchildren have input into the process. They will feel very proud when their ideas are used. And, if you have kids involved in scouts or other groups, remember that they are often looking for unusual items for craft projects.

When you've exhausted all ideas for the things you've found lying around your house, hold on to the rest of the items. You will need them in Steps 2 and 3.

Step 2: Look Before You Buy
Surely there is something you need this week that you are going to buy from the store. But before you buy a new make-up organizer, look to see if there is a spare tool or tackle box in the garage that will work instead. Look through your pile again to see if there is anything there that can be used. Can a coffee mug with a broken handle be used as a lipstick holder? How about as a catch all for hair clips or a handy container for cotton balls?

If you can find things that you already have that can be used instead of buying something, in addition to saving money, you will also be conserving our natural resources. For example, if you cut a toilet paper roll into three rings and cover them lengthwise with colored duct tape, you can make some pretty nifty napkin holders. These holders might not be the height of popular design, but they are a fun family project and, like duct tape, very serviceable. Recycling is more than dumping paper into a large bin; it is finding non-traditional uses for all kinds of items.

Step 3: Create a Mini Recycling Coop

Hopefully your pile of previously unwanted items is dwindling rapidly, but you are sure to have a lot of seemingly useless odds and ends left over. But, while something might be useless to you, it could be an item that is coveted by a neighbor.

This week, or as soon as scheduling allows, ask your friends and neighbors to do what you did in Step 1. If you are doing *Success Within* as a group, this will be a fabulous activity for all of you. Then schedule a date where you all get together, bringing all your leftovers to one central location. You will be surprised at the number of possessions your neighbors have and can't use that you have the perfect use for. This is a time to give, trade, and swap to your heart's content. It will give you a reason to spend time with people you love and care about in a fun, productive, and unusual way. Make it a pot-luck and munch your way through all sorts of surprises. If you want to make it a really big event, you could even get members of your church or fraternal organization involved.

Then, when everyone has picked over everything to their heart's content, sort the donate-able items from the trash, send one group to the dump and the other to the Salvation Army or Goodwill. At the end of the day, you will have had some great conversation, a truly unique experience and, hopefully, have found some very cool stuff.

Week 46 Success Plan

* Gather all unused, unusable, and useless items from your home
* Be creative and look for other ways to use these items
* Look within your home before you buy
* Join forces with a small group and have a swap day

Week 47

BALANCING ACT

"We can try to avoid making choices by doing nothing, but even that is a decision." —Gary Collins

Everyone has at one time or another wanted something so badly they'd do anything—or almost anything—to get it. While that amount of zeal can be admirable, in hindsight, those decisions are usually the ones that backfire. Not that it isn't a good idea, sometimes, to think with your heart, but for the decision to be sound, and for you to be without a shadow of a doubt, your head must also have some say-so in the decision making process. Common sense prevails this week as you weigh both sides of an important decision.

We all have to make decisions every day. From minor decisions such as what to wear and where to stop for coffee, to more important decisions such as where you will go to college or on vacation, or which house you will buy, the process affects our lives, and the lives of others, more than we can imagine.

Country star Clay Walker has had a life-long interest in horses. Had he not made the decision to pursue that interest, he never would have met his wife, Lori, who also loves horses.

John Wooden is the famed former UCLA basketball coach whose teams won ten collegiate championship titles in twelve years. He founded a basketball dynasty and many of his players, like Kareem Abdul-Jabbar, went on to become major forces in professional basketball. But before

Wooden went to UCLA, he had another offer from the University of Minnesota. Had Wooden chosen Minnesota over UCLA, it is very possible that the histories of both collegiate and professional basketball could have been much different. Just think of the number of lives that were affected by that one decision! Because we make so many decisions every day, it is important that we understand that the smallest decision we make can have a big impact on other people. When we think too much with our heart, or are so impulsive that we act without thinking at all, the consequences can be dire.

It is well known that in the late 1980s country outlaw Johnny PayCheck shot a man in an Ohio bar. That was probably a bad decision. John later served twenty-one months and admitted that the shooting was an impulsive one. He got mad, pulled out the gun and squeezed the trigger. Fortunately for everyone, the bullet just grazed the man's forehead, and he was not seriously injured.

Years ago after I had a vehicle stolen, I scraped together as much money as I could find at the time and bought the first five hundred dollar car that I came across. I knew I should have someone look at the engine, but I thought I couldn't afford it, so I bought the car "as is." A few days later my son and I were exiting off a Nashville freeway when we heard a series of loud "thunks." I looked in the rear view mirror to see dozens of engine parts flying from beneath the car. It was a veritable tornado of car parts and looked just like the scene in the *Wizard of Oz* where everything was flying by Dorothy's window, complete with a swirling gray haze, caused by the engine oil that was spewing behind us. Colby and I laugh about it now, but not having the car inspected was a bad, and expensive, decision. I couldn't afford to buy another car so Paul Overstreet and his wife, Julie, took pity on me and lent me one of their vehicles. I was, and am, very grateful to them, as it was more than a month before I could afford to buy another inexpensive car. But, I learned my lesson. This car I had inspected.

This week is all about balancing our hearts and heads to arrive at sound decisions—decisions so strong and so well made that you will not doubt that the decision you made was the right one. I really wanted (and needed) that five hundred dollar car, but I let my heart (and some desperation) overrule my head. I made my decision about the car in spite of my doubt, and that turned out not to be wise. This week you will find practical and realistic ways to obtain some of those "gotta have's," but you will use sound judgment and make the decision knowing just whom it will affect, and how.

Step 1: Identify a Decision in Your Life

You probably have at least one major decision to make in the next twelve months. Should you get a pet? Are you going to stay at your current job? Do you need to buy another car? Are you going to get married, divorced, or have a child? Will you be taking college classes anywhere, learning a new sport, or writing a book? Are you going to redecorate your home, landscape your yard, take a trip, or move across the country? How about changing churches, taking up a new hobby, or starting a small business?

Any of these, and countless others, qualify as a major decision. If you decide one way or the other without fully exploring the good and bad that go along with your decision, you could be in for more than a few surprises.

For this week, concentrate on just one decision you think you will be making in the next year.

Step 2: Pros and Cons

Once you have chosen something to make a decision about, get out a blank sheet of paper and draw a big fat line down the middle. On top and to the left of the line write the word Pros. On top and to the right of the line write Cons.

Now find a quiet spot and think of all the plusses and minuses involved in this decision. For example, if you are contemplating switching to a different job, in the Pros column you could list more money, bigger office, prestigious title, and one step closer to dream job. In the Cons column you might list longer hours, more time away from family, and would have to give up coaching soccer.

Remember to also list the pros and cons of how you will facilitate the decision. If you decide to purchase another car, how will you pay for it? Do you have money saved or will you need financing? If you are financing the car, what are the pros and cons of adding the payment to your monthly budget? If you decide to move, just how will you accomplish it? Are you moving yourself, or hiring a moving company, and what are the pros and cons of each?

Step 3: Visualize Both Sides

After you have listed as many pros and cons as you can think of, visualize both sides of the decision. If you are thinking of adding a puppy to the family, visualize the warm, wet puppy licks, and the years of enjoyment and companionship the dog will bring to your family. Do not forget, however, to visualize the costs of dog food, toys and vet bills. Remember to see the slippers the puppy has chewed and the dark, wet spot on the carpet when the puppy just could not wait another second. Be sure to list all of these visuals with your other pros and cons.

Step 4: Talk to Those the Decision Affects

On the back of your paper, list everyone you can possibly think of who will be affected by the decision. If you are thinking of moving, obviously everyone in your household will be affected (be sure to include pets on your list). If the move puts you closer to, or further away, from friends or relatives, they will be somewhat affected by the move as well, so add them to the list. Depending on how far you are thinking of moving, any social activities you have or charitable work you do may also be involved.

Once you have thought of as many people and situations as you can, sit down and discuss your idea with the people who will be the most affected. If you are moving across the country for a bigger and better job, your family might tell you that they do not care about the increase in salary as much as they do about not seeing you as often. Your family might also have other reasons why this move is not good from their standpoint. Make note of all their thoughts on the pros and cons list.

Step 5: Tally Up

Finally, look at the decision objectively. Are there many more pros than cons? Do the images you visualized lean more toward a plus or minus? And how about the other people involved in this decision: do they have strong feelings one way or another?

The evidence indicating the correct decision for you to make should be right there in front of you. But if the decision is still a close one, or if you have only a few things on one side but those things are very compelling, you may wish to add a ranking of one to five to each item you have listed. For instance, if you are thinking of getting married and you really, really, really love your intended, give that item a ranking of five on the Pros side. If, on the other side of the coin, your family and friends are kind of lukewarm about your betrothed, give that item a ranking of three in the Cons column. Continue on until every item you have listed, including all the visualization and all the thoughts and feelings of people who are affected, have been ranked. Then tally up each side and the numbers should weigh out, one way or another.

If, no matter what you do, the pros and cons and the numbers come out fairly even, it is possible that you do not have enough information to make an intelligent decision. Go back and find more ways that this decision will affect your life in both positive and negative ways.

Once your decision has been made, you can feel confident that you utilized all the information you had to make the best decision you could. You'll just have to let fate and the future take it from here.

* Plan to make one specific and major decision in your life
* Make a list of the pros and cons of the prospective decision
* Visualize both sides of the decision
* Talk with those whom the decision affects
* Assign a number value to the items on your pro and con lists
* Get more information if necessary

Week 48

PAUSE FOR POISE

"The key to winning is poise under stress."
—Paul Brown

Having poise means being comfortable in your own skin. It's being self-confident and composed in virtually any situation, under every possible difficult condition; it is freedom from affectation or embarrassment no matter what the circumstances. Poise is the ultimate grace under pressure, and is important to have because we think best when we are focused, rather than when we are stressed or angry. And, one of the best qualities you can have in a difficult situation is focus.

Poise comes from two things: being self-assured in all that you do, and feeling good about yourself. Life deals us all kinds of difficult situations, from those that make us nervous to those that make us impatient, angry or afraid. It is how you conduct yourself during these times, that is the real test of who you are. This week you will push yourself a little and display one of the hardest attributes to show in life. Poise.

What kinds of situations make you feel completely comfortable? Are you at ease around home and family, or is that the kind of situation that makes you a little nervous? If so, you are not alone. Many people live in dysfunctional families, and if you are one of them it's good to remember that the only actions you can completely control are your own. If you stay above the fray, then maybe some of the others will choose to follow.

What other areas make you feel out of place? When you are at work? In public places? In crowds? Going to a party? Going to the dentist? Meeting new people? When you are called on to perform? Numerous polls have shown that public speaking makes a huge number of people feel uncomfortable. I know many celebrities who feel very much at home on stage, but when they have to talk to a small group of people, they become so frightened they make themselves physically ill.

Hospitals and other medical settings also tend to make people feel uncomfortable and nervous. I used to date a physician, and I do not think he has any real understanding of the blatant fear most people experience when confronted with a medical procedure or emergency. The fear is often rooted in the ignorance of us non-medical types. Those who work in medicine have years of training that give them an understanding of any given situation, while we do not know if the person we are dealing with is competent, or how serious the medical issue really is. And then there is all the mind-boggling paperwork to deal with. We could be signing our children away and not even realize it.

Family holidays can also be stressful. Too much family togetherness spent with relatives we rarely see during other times of the year can cause the best of us to snap. Many emergency room personnel are on special alert during holidays, because they know that all the stress can lead to serious medical problems like heart attack and stroke, and that a small family spat can easily turn into a real Hatfield and McCoy type feud.

I mention all of these situations because when we are afraid, impatient, nervous, or angry, good behavior is often the last thing on our minds. Poise and confidence fly out the window as we lose our temper, snap at those around us, or so totally lose all thought that we just stop and stare. At nothing.

Before I began working with Marty Haggard, he had suffered a traumatic brain injury in an auto accident. I hooked Marty up as a spokesperson for a nationally known brain injury foundation and Marty began doing interviews on the long-term difficulties people with brain injuries face. When Tennessee was considering a bicycle helmet law, Marty testified at a senate sub-committee hearing in Knoxville. Before his presentation, Marty was so nervous that I thought he was going to throw up. We wandered around the huge lobby in the government office building and whenever people would head his way, Marty would duck behind a pillar. Right then, dealing with both people and his impending presentation was just one situation too much.

When Marty began his presentation he said a few words and then stopped and stared at the fifty or so people in the room. I truly thought the experience was so overwhelming for him that he was going to walk out the door. But Marty then took a deep breath, put down his notes, and spoke very eloquently for twenty minutes about his own injury and relayed stories of several brain injured people he had since met. He wrapped his presentation with a moving plea to the sub-committee for more funding for brain injury prevention and rehabilitation. In all my years as a publicist, that was one of my proudest moments. Marty was obviously terrified at the task ahead of him, but he dug deep within himself and found an incredible amount of poise. He presented an elegant and focused statement, and did an awesome job.

This week you, too, will find poise in difficult situations as you stretch yourself, and create opportunities to be the very best *you* that you can be.

Step 1: Put Yourself in the Path of Poise

It can be a real test of honor and ability when you attempt to keep your composure in difficult situations. This week, intentionally put yourself in a situation that makes you angry, impatient, nervous or afraid. Notice that the word danger is not included. You do not need to do anything dangerous to develop poise.

What makes you act less than your best? Is it family bickering that lowers you to a screaming match? Remember, it takes two to have a fight. Instead of losing your temper, pull out your poise and present your side of the issue calmly, clearly and concisely. If the other person refuses to listen, distance yourself for a while until tempers have cooled.

Paul Overstreet knows that I am afraid of heights. Whenever I am confronted with anything higher than the back of a horse, I become very nervous and unfocused. I certainly am not at my best. My only thought is to get back down to ground level as quickly as possible. On the occasions I flew with Paul and his band, he made sure I had a window seat. All I could think of during any of those trips was what I would do when I was sucked out the window. Yet I still had to learn to focus on business and be pleasant to those around me. When we had to go to the Secretary of State office for something and ended up on the "twenty-somethingth" floor, Paul pulled me over to the floor to ceiling windows and forced me to stand there while we talked to the people in the office. I was sure I would fall out of those windows any second and was trying to figure out whether it was better to land on my side or curled up in a ball while we talked corporate business.

I don't know if anyone other than Paul noticed my discomfort. I hope I had enough poise that they did not. Since then I have forced myself into enough terrifyingly high positions that my knees are no longer weak. I usually can breathe normally and if you look into my eyes, you no longer see the expression of a trapped animal. When I recently flew to Tampa, I chose a window seat, and even enjoyed most of the trip.

I had to dig for poise through my fear. You may have to find yours by holding your tongue at family gatherings, by finding yet more patience with a slow child, or by confronting your nervousness in crowds. Only by overcoming your fears, can you move closer to becoming the best you that you can be. This week, choose one situation that makes you nervous, impatient, angry or afraid. Be sure to enlist the help of a friend, or a group of friends, if you need extra moral support.

Step 2: Confront the Issue

Whatever specific fear you chose, make plans to put yourself in the middle of that kind of a situation as soon as possible. Prepare for this by visualizing the situation repeatedly and thoroughly. What people are around you? Where is this taking place? What time of day is it? What are you wearing? Include as many details as possible. If crowds make you nervous, make plans to go to the mall at a crowded time and smile at the shoppers. If all you can do this first time is sit on a bench for five minutes, that's great! You are there. Stay relaxed by taking deep breaths. Take a friend to support you, if needed. When you walk out, allow yourself to feel triumphant! You did it and next time you will stay longer and do even better.

If you are intimidated around your boss and have a job review coming up, visualize the expected details of the review and watch yourself as you sit with poise and confidence. If you get flustered talking to your boss, instead of looking him in the eye, or looking at the ground, try focusing on the top of his nose—at the point right between the eyes. Unless the other person is less than a foot away, they will perceive you as being very confident, as they will think you are looking them right in the eye.

Step 3: Repeat Often
Continue to pull out your poise whenever you are confronted with a situation that puts you at less than your best. Take a moment and a deep breath and remember to stay calm and focused. The more you do this, the more confident you will become, and the better—and more poised—you will be.

Week 48 Success Plan

* Create a situation that will make you dig for your poise
* Visualize the event ahead of time
* Enlist the support of friends
* Start small
* Repeat with longer and tougher situations

Week 49

SOMETIMES LIFE SUCKS

"Expect the best, plan for the worst, and prepare to be surprised."
—Denis Waitley

Sometimes life is just the pits. But in the words of Coach John Wooden, "Those who have never suffered adversity never know the meaning of true success." Hard times do make you stronger, but getting through them can be incredibly tough. People, for the most part, do not think rationally when an emergency arises, so this week involves developing a crisis plan and learning to enlist the aid of those closest to you, just in case the worst should ever happen.

In the past three months I have learned of three young men who have died in tragic auto accidents. This is a horrible trend no matter how you look at it, but what made it a little easier for one family was a crisis plan. This one family, unlike the other two, had a plan they had developed in case of just such a catastrophe. Their plan had delegated certain members certain duties, such as calling other relatives, with back up people for each item on the plan.

What would you and your family do if, say, your home burned to the ground? Do you have several escape routes from each room? Have you designated a safe meeting place for all family members? Do several people know which insurance agent to call? Where will you stay after the fire? As awful as it is to talk about things like this, it is much worse not to have a plan in place in case something does happen.

If the adults in your family are all at the hospital dealing with an emergency, who watches the kids? If an intruder enters your home in the middle of the night, does each member of the family know what to do? If you lock your self out of the house, do you have a back up plan? What do you do in case of a tornado or hurricane, or if the power is off?

These and an infinite number of other emergencies can happen at any time. Since my son was small, we have had a plan for every scenario we can think of, including nuclear holocaust. Rather than making us feel morbid, or being upset about all the negative possibilities, our plan has given us both a sense of security. If something happens, we each know what we need to do.

Members of the family I mentioned earlier—the family who had a crisis plan—recently told me that having a plan gave them a sense of order and kept tension to a minimum. In their grief, each had specific jobs to do. The jobs kept each family member busy and functioning in the midst of terrible shock. Nothing anyone could do would bring back their brother and son, but the family could stay focused on all the many things they had to do in organizing the funeral and notifying friends and relatives, because there was a plan. Additionally, because the family was so organized, additional mini disasters were avoided. You know the kind. You are just barely coping with some terrible crisis in life and then you realize you are out of milk. That single little crisis can send you over the fine line between barely coping, and completely losing it.

In addition to having a plan, it is important to have a support team. If your family is called out of town suddenly for a funeral, who can you call on to feed the cat and dog? Who will look in on your place? If your car breaks down and you can't pick up your children from daycare before it closes, who can you call to go get your kids? If you break your leg and can't drive for a few weeks, who will take you to the doctor and to the grocery store? It is very important to enlist the aid of friends and neighbors in your emergency plan, and most will be glad to help.

I once worked with a client whose best friend and benefactor was dying of cancer. My client stayed at the hospital for three or four days helping to care for his dying friend, but eventually had to go out of town. Very late one night, I received a call from the hospital saying that the friend was asking for my client and probably wouldn't last until morning. But when I called my client on his cell phone to let him know, he apparently was out of range. But, in case this exact possibility arose, he had developed a plan. He had given me a list of people to call who might be able to track him down, including the number for the Wyoming State Highway Patrol, the state my client was to be traveling through late that night.

By now, it was three in the morning. I called everyone on the list and asked him or her to have my client call the hospital if they heard from him. The dispatcher at the state patrol was especially helpful. I gave her the plate numbers from my missing client's vehicle, and within thirty minutes, a trooper had located him.

I was a little amazed that not one person on this list was angry for being awakened by a stranger in the middle of the night. Everyone wanted to help. Sometimes, all you have to do is ask.

This week you will create a crisis plan for your own home and family. Hopefully you will never have cause to implement it. But if you do, this plan will make your life much, much easier.

Step 1: Make a Disaster List
This is something you can do alone, or with the assistance of your family. Most people, including kids, feel far safer and more secure, in knowing there is a plan for virtually every situation. Think of every possibility that could befall your family and write it down: falls, heart attacks, strokes, fires, burglaries, lost keys, car breakdowns, storms, the works. Think of everything you possibly can.

Step 2: Develop a Plan for Each Item
Now think of a plan for each item. For fires you should develop escape routes from each room and designate a safe, central meeting place outside the home that all family members can find. All children should know what to do if they are home alone and mommy or daddy or grandma or grandpa gets sick. Every person on Earth should know basic first aid. Each member of the family should know where extra keys are hidden and should be able to be reached in case disaster does strike.

When I jumped off the back of my truck and hurt my knee a few years ago, my son knew immediately to get the phone and also to bring the crutches from their corner in the basement. He was a Boy Scout and knew just what first aid principles to apply. As the injured person, it was a huge relief for me to know that someone was there who could help.

Step 3: Enlist Aid

Now fill the holes in your plan with friends and neighbors. If your family has to be away, who picks up the mail? Who picks up the kids if you cannot? Who takes you to work if you cannot drive? As mentioned earlier, most people are happy to be "on call" and it's wonderful to know you have people you can count on, and more importantly, who can count on you.

As my son was not yet driving when I hurt my knee, I called my friend Jolene, who was the first person on my list of three to call in case of injury. She was happy to drop everything and spend close to twenty-four hours with me in the emergency room at the hospital. And later, when I had surgery, my mother was able to fly in from Minnesota and spend three weeks. As I could not drive for eight weeks, I called on a number of neighbors and friends to help out. All were people I had talked to years previously about the possibility of helping in an emergency, and all are people whom I would drop everything for if the roles were ever reversed.

People want to help you. Explain what you are doing and ask if they can pitch in, in the unlikely event of an emergency. Be sure to let people know that you would do the same for them.

Step 4: File the Plan in a Convenient Place

Everyone in your household needs to know where your written emergency plan is stored. It could be in a kitchen drawer, a filing cabinet, or taped to the basement wall. And, it needs to be reviewed and updated several times a year. The Boy Scout motto is "Be Prepared." I have found that if you follow that advice, you can usually keep your head above water in the worst of circumstances.

Week 49 Success Plan

* Develop an emergency plan
* List every disaster you can think of
* Make a plan for each item
* If you do not know basic first aid, take a class
* Enlist the potential aid of others
* Store your plan where everyone can find it
* Review and update it frequently

FOLLOWING THROUGH

"Only put off until tomorrow what you are willing to die having left undone." —Pablo Picasso

People have so many wonderful ideas . . . then nothing happens. It's called follow through, or lack of it. Nothing happens without it. Whether intentionally not done or accidentally forgotten, those loose ends are critical to success in any way, shape, or form.

·   In the public relations business we have what I call "throw away" press releases. These releases usually detail a relatively unimportant event in the life of a celebrity and are not followed up with individual phone calls or emails to the media, as are the major releases that are sent out.

Early in my public relations career, I sent a release out nationally about a concert Johnny PayCheck was giving to inmates at an Arizona prison. This concert was part of the community service work that was required in John's release from prison. We had sent a lot of releases in months previous to this about other service work John had done, so I classified this as a throw away—send it out and hope a few members of the press use it before they throw it away. We also had other announcements we were planning to send about John's career in the next few weeks, so I sent this one earlier than I normally would have. This was back in the days when we were still mailing releases, so publicists had to think a little further in advance—to allow for slow delivery times—than they do now. But in this instance I found that a long lead and a short memory can be a little scary.

A number of uneventful weeks went by. Then one morning John called and was furious with his manager. "I can't work with him. I swear I'm going to get rid of him," cried John.

Then the manager called and was raving mad at John. And so it went back and forth a few times before I had the sense to have my assistant tell both of them I was out of the office.

On my drive home I always listened to *ABC National News* on the radio, which came on right at five o'clock. I was on the freeway, just west of Nashville, and thinking about the anger that Johnny and his manager had for each other when the teaser for that evening's broadcast came on. The first teaser was about raging fires in California, the second was about trouble in the mid-East and the third was, "Legendary Johnny PayCheck goes back to prison."

My first response was to drive into the ditch, where I proceeded to beat my head against the steering wheel. I just knew John had killed his manager. He had threatened to do it that morning when he said, "I'm going to get rid of him." At the time, I thought John was talking about firing his manager, not killing him!

By the time I had calmed down enough to listen to the radio, the ads were finished and John's story was on. Imagine my relief when I realized the teaser was a cute headline for John's concert at the Arizona prison. What I had considered throw away material was actually a headline story on national news, and of course John meant he was going to explore different arrangements for management, which he did several months later.

While I drove the rest of the way home, I thought of all the opportunities we had missed by not following up on that one press release. If ABC radio had used it as a headline story, chances are that other media would have used it prominently, too, if only we had followed up the release with a simple phone call.

While my lack of follow-up with the press release was a miscalculation in the importance of the release, there are a number of people who intentionally do not follow through– –in other words, they make commitments and then do not fulfill the obligation they made. Every time you agree to do something small (calling a friend at a prearranged time, running an errand), or something large (exclusivity in a relationship, a financial obligation, delivering a proposal on time) you are making a commitment. When you break commitments you disappoint the people around you and inconvenience people who are relying on you. If you cannot follow through on a commitment, you probably shouldn't have made it in the first place. Of course, if there are unusual circumstances that prevent your follow through, a simple phone call to the people involved should release you from your obligation.

There are many other reasons for not following through on something. One is habit, as there are many people who rarely finish anything they start. I am sure you know a few people like this. Other times people get busy; life intervenes and we get distracted. I've also known several people who don't follow through because they have an inner fear of success: if they follow through and complete something, it might not turn out exactly right. Better to slack off and not really try, they reason, than risk doing the job and failing.

Unfortunately, people with this type of fear do not realize that there is much to be learned in events not turning out exactly as planned.

You, on the other hand, do understand that. You are very close to finishing a very extensive program and I am sure have had many successes and failures along the way, yet you persevered. You've spent the past weeks expanding your horizons and enriching your life. But there are probably several areas that were, for whatever reason, left unfinished. This week you will go back through *Success Within* and do your own follow up on a few of these "leftovers."

Step 1: Review Loose Ends

Flip through *Success Within* and your *Success Within* notebook, and jot down the specific steps you did not finish. Or, if you finished everything, maybe there is some element that you implemented in your life for a while and planned to continue, but it got lost in everything else you are doing. For example, did you stay on the budget you made in Week 29? Have you continued to put six people up every day as in Week 14? Are you still speaking as positively as you were in Week 19?

This week is time for you to do a quick review of the entire *Success Within* program, renew your efforts to follow through on steps you did not finish, and recommit to ideas you wanted to keep in your life, but that have fallen by the wayside.

Step 2: Take it Outside

There very possibly are other areas in your life in which you do not follow up as thoroughly as needed, if at all. Think about your work. How many people should you have called back last week, but didn't? How many little odds and ends are on your plate and have been there for months? Sometimes little things can pile up into such an overwhelming mound that none of the tasks ever get done. But just think how much more productive you would be if you could finally clear all of those items off your to do list. All it takes is a few minutes a day of strict attention to detail. Before you know it, it all will be done.

At home, have you repeatedly promised your kids or grandchildren that you'd take them on an outing, but you have not yet gone? Did you begin a redecorating project two months ago and never finish?

When I was growing up, I had a friend whose father began remodeling their living room. This was when we were twelve. When I came to visit during winter break of my second year in college, he still had not finished. For eight years, they had a never-ending series of drywall and wall joists balanced around the television. There were numerous toolboxes, cans of nails, and hammers and saws dotting the perimeter of the room. My friend's father obviously had a serious lack of follow-through, and since my last visit I've often wondered if he ever did finish the job. My guess is that almost thirty years later the room is still in some sort of disarray.

This week, in addition to following up on unfinished *Success Within* business, take your follow-up skills outside *Success Within* and follow through on some of the things that have been hanging on the fringes of your life. In addition to now having more time for other activities, you will feel absolutely wonderful that you completed those tasks.

Week 50 Success Plan

* Review any loose ends in *Success Within*
* Commit to reestablishing some of the elements of *Success Within* in your life
* Follow up by completing odds and ends at work and at home
* Commit to following up more consistently in the future

Week 51

JUST CHILL

"A good rest is half the work."
—Slovenian Proverb

After working on *Success Within* so hard for so long you will fall most likely into one of two categories. The first is filled with people who, now that they have gotten in the habit of accomplishing so much, see all that they have done and can't wait to do even more. In the other group, people are more than ready for a little rest. Depending on which group you fall into, this week will be incredibly easy or terribly difficult. You see, like the television show *Seinfeld*, this week is all about the active pursuit of nothing.

No matter how hard you work, or don't work, everyone needs a break now and then. This is that week. But there are different kinds of ways to take that break, and different ways to do absolutely nothing.

Here are two scenarios. The first person spends one day doing absolutely nothing. At the end of the day he or she really can't recall how that time was spent. The second person, however, spent an hour on the front porch in the morning, just staring into the distance. But while they were sitting and staring, they were listening to the beautiful music sung by the birds. They were enjoying the brisk morning air, and watching the sunlight as it filtered through the trees. Then they lay for a time in a hammock, breathed deeply, and listened to the wind rustle the leaves above them. After that they sent out for pizza and watched a funny movie on TV with several friends.

The difference? The first person might have done nothing, which was the goal of this exercise. But the second person found many ways to enjoy doing nothing.

For most people, it is very difficult to find time to do nothing. We are all so busy we view down time as time that is wasted. But everyone needs to recharge his or her batteries sometime. Consider a battery for a cell phone. It goes and goes and goes for quite a long time. Then one day it is slow to function. A few minutes later it begins beeping a distress signal. Then it doesn't work at all. But, if you recharge that battery, it is as good as new. If you look at doing nothing from that perspective—that it is something your body and mind need in order to be able to accomplish even more--then maybe this won't be so hard to do after all.

Finding time to do nothing can be the most difficult part of the task, so you have to treat it as you would anything else and schedule the time. Maybe you can rearrange your schedule so you can take an entire day and do nothing. Or maybe it is easier to take a few hours every few days.

Let's say you block Tuesday evening; everyone is out of your house then anyway. What will you do? There are two rules to this, you can't plan anything, and however you spend your time, you have to enjoy it. But why no plans? If you plan something, when the actual moment comes you may not feel like doing that exact thing, but because you planned it, you feel you have to do it. Even if you don't end up doing what you had planned, there will be some part of you that will feel guilty because you are doing something else. Many of us need to give ourselves permission to have fun, and let's face it; guilt does take the enjoyment out of life.

So, no plans. But, what will you find to do? Whatever strikes you at that moment. You could take an aimless walk, sit by the fire and think of spring, watch the traffic, go to a museum, go to the mall, take a nap, or meditate. You could even be a closet couch potato and end up spending your time doing nothing but flipping channels from the recliner. If you enjoy it and it is unplanned, that's great. As long as you are not doing anything that remotely resembles work or household chores, you are doing well.

One thing you will probably find: at first your mind will be very cluttered and it will be hard to slow everything down so you can enjoy doing nothing. So, while you are busy not doing anything at all, try not to think of anything important. Just be in the moment and enjoy the sights and sounds around you. This process of clearing your mind might take several minutes. Or it might take weeks of practice, depending on how active and busy you usually are. If you find this especially hard, keep in mind the battery analogy and know that your internal batteries desperately need this rest period, as well as the fact that after your brief period of "recharging" you will be able to get so much more done than usual, you will surprise even yourself.

Many years ago I had a business partner who worked eighteen hours a day, seven days a week. Monetarily, he was very successful, and he was relentless in his quest for detail, never leaving anything left undone before turning in for the night. I worried that he was going to work himself into the ground so I was very glad to hear he was planning a two-week vacation with his new wife and her family.

I smelled trouble, however, when, on the day before he left, he handed me his itinerary. Expecting to see the cities he would be in on a given day, I was surprised instead to see in addition to the expected information, a timetable for each day. The day after he was arriving at Cousin Jen's in Montana, for instance, he and his wife were rising at 6:30 A.M. He allowed thirty minutes for them to shower and prepare for the day. Then from 7:00 to 7:25, they were eating breakfast. He allowed five minutes for them to walk from the house to the stables where from 7:30 to 7:45, they would be bringing the horses in from the pasture. And so on the day––and the entire vacation—went. Imagine why I was not surprised when later in the year he announced that his wife was divorcing him. He couldn't figure it out, but I knew just what the problem was. He could do pretty much anything he set his mind to, but he had no idea how to do absolutely nothing.

Step 1: Clear Your Calendar

Before you can make your first attempt at doing absolutely nothing, you need to make time for this big, new adventure. This week, rearrange whatever you need to clear a few hours. If you are not all that busy this week, that's even better for you. The more time you can devote to this, the more time you have to recharge. Be sure to clue your family in so you are not interrupted in the middle of doing nothing. It's hard to reenergize if people are constantly pulling at you.

Step 2: Do Nothing

Once your schedule includes a block of time specifically for doing nothing and the moment finally arrives, what will you do? Simply whatever strikes your fancy at that moment.

Remember, no plans, just whatever you feel like doing—or not doing. Clear your brain of all thoughts that involve work, family problems, or errands. This is your time. Make the most of it and enjoy doing nothing at all.

Week 51 Success Plan

* Clear your calendar
* Find absolutely nothing to do
* Clear your brain
* Relax and enjoy the good life

Week 52

COME ON AND CELEBRATE!

"The more you praise and celebrate your life, the more there is in life to celebrate." —Oprah Winfrey

Congratulations! In just a few minutes, you will have successfully completed all the steps to creating great moments in your life. You will have found the true success that is inside you in helping others, pushing yourself toward new challenges, and in giving back. I am sure that there have been some wonderful moments in the last fifty-one weeks, and now it's time to embrace and celebrate each one of them with your family and friends at a party. And guess what? You are the guest of honor.

Choose a convenient day and throw the party of your dreams. It does not have to be elaborate; the best parties are memorable because of the people who attend them, not because of the food or where they are held. Your Success Party could be a picnic or a potluck, a chips and dip reception, or a catered meal. You could hold it at your home, the home of a friend, or even in a restaurant, church, or a city park.

The most important part of the party is to include as many people who were a part of your *Success Within* journey as possible. Your family will be there, of course, because they were closely affected by all of your *Success Within* activities, then any friends and neighbors who helped you. And remember all the people you helped, or who helped you. They all should be invited. If you got to know someone of a different faith or generation, they should be there. If you became involved in a charitable cause, invite the new friends you made through that organization. Everyone and anyone who was the smallest part of your success should be invited.

If you wanted to go all out on the party, you could honor everyone with a small gift, a candle, or a hand written note expressing your appreciation. You could fill the room with balloons and streamers. Or you could just give everyone a warm hug. Unfortunately, not everyone will be able to attend, but choose a day that seems available for as many people as possible.

Your Success Party is all about sharing your newfound success with your friends. People who were important to you along the way should be recognized at this event and applauded. Bring them up to the front of the room and tell everyone how this person changed your life. Actually, you should share with everyone there the many wonderful moments you have had in the past year, or two, or three. Not everyone gets through *Success Within* in fifty-two weeks. Many people go over certain weeks two or even three times, until they have fully experienced all that week has in store for them. And even though I have been living this for close to thirty years, I regularly go back over a particular section or exercise. One, because I have so much fun with it; and two, because it keeps my priorities in life in line.

But before you have your party and close the cover on this book for the final time there are several things I'd like you to do. The first is to update your dreams, desires and goals lists. Hopefully you have crossed off many of the items you initially listed because you have already done them. You may, however, find that your goals and interests have changed over the past year. Maybe it is no longer important to you to climb Mt. Everest, or sail around the world. Instead, maybe you would rather hike the Himalayas, or just stay home and enjoy the many people who surround your life.

Be sure to decorate your new list just as much as you did the old. Besides it being a creative outlet, it is far more fun to put a gold star by something you have accomplished––or cross it completely off your list—if the list is decorated with yarn, glitter, or pictures.

And by the way, just how many things from your lists did you accomplish this year? You may have completed a great many or just a few. It doesn't matter. What does matter are the many great moments you have had, all the new people you have brought in to your life, and the many people who have shared any part of this walk with you.

The second thing I'd like you to do is to remember that *Success Within*, which is really all the many gifts you have to give to the world, does not stop with the closing of this book. You have every day of the rest of your life to enjoy, to make others smile, to help people with their troubles, and to teach new friends new skills. You have every day of your life to learn, to grow as a person, and to reach every goal you have ever set for yourself. You have the rest of your life to find all that you ever wanted.

So as you go about the many days that are still ahead of you, remember the steps in *Success Within*. If you come across someone who can benefit from something you've learned here, please pass it on. Please share your knowledge and your experiences as you continue to create and enjoy the greatest moments of your life.

Lastly, please take a moment to re-cap the past twelve weeks.

1. What did you determine about your own character in Week 40? How about the character of those around you?

2. In Week 41, how well were you able to streamline your day? How much extra time were you able to create? What strengths did you determine you have? And what weaknesses?

3. What acts of consideration were you able to do in Week 42? How did you feel when the task was completed? Have you been able to provide any acts of consideration since that week?

4. What were the three biggest changes in your life as discussed in Week 43? How did those specific changes alter the course of your life? Can you look back and see that the changes were ultimately for the better? Did you toss out any old traditions, or create any new ones?

5. In Week 44 did you find a person to mentor? What, specifically, have you done in your mentoring relationship? How has the mentoring relationship added to your life?

6. What books did you find to read in Week 45? How well did you like reading outside your comfort zone? Were you able to introduce another person to the world of books? If so, who?

7. In Week 46, how many alternative uses for items did you find? Which object was put to the most unusual

use? What did you do with the things you could find no use for?

8. What major decision did you concentrate on in Week 47? After you went through the Pros and Cons process, was the right decision clear to you? How did this process help you make the decision? Do you think the decision you made would have been different had you not used this method?

9. What uncomfortable situation did you put yourself in during Week 48? Did confronting your fear help you overcome it? How many times since then have you pushed yourself to do something similar?

10. Did your family and friends help you with your disaster plan in Week 49? What events did you plan for that you would not otherwise have thought of? Have you been able to help a friend with their plan for disaster?

11. What loose ends did you tie up in Week 50? Had you forgotten about the item, or had it been nagging in the back of your mind? How long did it take you to tie up the loose end?

12. In Week 51, what did you do when you "did nothing"? How easy was it for you to accomplish this? Have you been able to schedule regular times to recharge?

SUCCESS PLAN
FOR THE REST OF YOUR LIFE
★

Throw a huge bash and invite everyone who was a part of your *Success Within* story. At the party, introduce everyone whom you met through your *Success Within* experiences, and share your best success stories with the crowd.

Update your dreams, desires and goals not just today, but on a regular basis. As you go through your life, you will grow and change with your many experiences. As a result, your goals may change. So update your lists regularly—whether it is every few months or just once a year—and refer to them often. Years down the road you will be able to look back and remember all the fabulous adventures you had while accomplishing more than you ever dreamed you could.

Share your experiences. If you had an especially moving *Success Within* moment (or moments) be sure to tell others who could benefit from the story. One of the most rewarding things you will ever do is give someone a piece of information that changes their life for the better, or give them a tool that is helpful in getting through a rough time.

Continue to create great moments in your life. Remember that *Success Within* never stops, because it is all about the success that is already inside you.

AFTERWORD

*

If you completed the entire *Success Within* program, know that I am extraordinarily proud of you. You know that what you have accomplished is truly mind-boggling. But if you have only done a few weeks of *Success Within*, know that I am proud of you, as well. There are gifts for you to give and receive in any week, in any order, and I am tremendously honored that any of you chose to spend part of your life with *Success Within*. I am especially excited because every one of you is much closer to being the very best *you* that you can possibly be.

If you have an especially moving *Success Within* story, I'd love to hear about it. I do not know at this point what will be done with anything that you as a reader might send me, but who knows, if there are enough great stories out there, maybe there will be another book. If there is, we'll be sure to contact you for permission to use your story. When sending stories, please email them to me at lisawysocky@comcast.net. Be sure to include your name, address, phone number and email address. Please also check for the latest updates at www.successwithinbook.com.

In closing, I'd like to wish each of you a life filled with extraordinary people, and many wonderful experiences that you will treasure forever.

Lisa Wysocky
April 2005

ABOUT THE AUTHOR
★

Lisa Wysocky is the Owner of White Horse Enterprises, Inc., where she works as a publicist, music industry manager, and editor. When a knee injury cut short Lisa's career as a horse trainer, she ventured into her second love, music. Her talent with quality, biographical, and promotional material piloted her career into a self-owned public-relations firm. A motivational public speaker, Lisa has spoken to countless organizations. Lisa is also the author of *The Power of Horses: True Stories from Country Music Stars* (Fura Books, 2002). Lisa lives in Nashville, Tennessee with her son.

PHOTO CREDIT:
FARRIS L. POOLE
STUDIO 10 NASHVILLE